THE
SOCIAL SECURITY
& MEDICARE
HANDBOOK

WHAT YOU NEED TO
KNOW EXPLAINED SIMPLY

BY V.R. LEONARD

The Social Security and Medicare Handbook: What You Need to
Know Explained Simply

Copyright © 2008 by Atlantic Publishing Group, Inc.
1405 SW 6th Ave. • Ocala, Florida 34471 • 800-814-1132 • 352-622-1875–Fax
Web site: www.atlantic-pub.com • E-mail: sales@atlantic-pub.com
SAN Number: 268-1250

ISBN-13: 978-1-60138-132-3   ISBN-10: 1-60138-132-8

Library of Congress Cataloging-in-Publication Data

Leonard, V. R. (Vaughnlea R.), 1969-
  The social security and medicare handbook : what you need to know explained simply / by
V.R. Leonard.
     p. cm.
  Includes bibliographical references and index.
  ISBN-13: 978-1-60138-132-3 (alk. paper)
  ISBN-10: 1-60138-132-8 (alk. paper)
  1. Social security--Law and legislation--United States--Popular works. 2. Medicare--Law and
legislation--Popular works. 3. Old age pensions--Law and legislation--United States--Popular
works. 4. Insurance, Disability--Law and legislation--United States--Popular works. I. Title.

KF3650.L46 2008
344.7302'26--dc22

                                        2008012675

INTERIOR LAYOUT DESIGN: Vickie Taylor • vtaylor@atlantic-pub.com

Printed on Recycled Paper

Printed in the United States

We recently lost our beloved pet "Bear," who was not only
our best and dearest friend but also the "Vice President of
Sunshine" here at Atlantic Publishing. He did not receive
a salary but worked tirelessly 24 hours a day to please
his parents. Bear was a rescue dog that turned around
and showered myself, my wife Sherri, his grandparents
Jean, Bob and Nancy and every person and animal he met
(maybe not rabbits) with friendship and love. He made a
lot of people smile every day.

We wanted you to know that a portion of the profits of this
book will be donated to The Humane Society of
the United States.

–Douglas & Sherri Brown

THE HUMANE SOCIETY
OF THE UNITED STATES ©

The human-animal bond is as old as human history. We cherish our animal companions for their unconditional affection and acceptance. We feel a thrill when we glimpse wild creatures in their natural habitat or in our own backyard.

Unfortunately, the human-animal bond has at times been weakened. Humans have exploited some animal species to the point of extinction.

The Humane Society of the United States makes a difference in the lives of animals here at home and worldwide. The HSUS is dedicated to creating a world where our relationship with animals is guided by compassion. We seek a truly humane society in which animals are respected for their intrinsic value, and where the human-animal bond is strong.

Want to help animals? We have plenty of suggestions. Adopt a pet from a local shelter, join The Humane Society and be a part of our work to help companion animals and wildlife. You will be funding our educational, legislative, investigative and outreach projects in the U.S. and across the globe.

Or perhaps you'd like to make a memorial donation in honor of a pet, friend or relative? You can through our Kindred Spirits program. And if you'd like to contribute in a more structured way, our Planned Giving Office has suggestions about estate planning, annuities, and even gifts of stock that avoid capital gains taxes.

Maybe you have land that you would like to preserve as a lasting habitat for wildlife. Our Wildlife Land Trust can help you. Perhaps the land you want to share is a backyard—that's enough. Our Urban Wildlife Sanctuary Program will show you how to create a habitat for your wild neighbors.

So you see, it's easy to help animals. And The HSUS is here to help.

The Humane Society of the United States
2100 L Street NW
Washington, DC 20037
202-452-1100
www.hsus.org

TABLE OF CONTENTS

PREFACE

WHAT YOU NEED TO KNOW, EXPLAINED SIMPLY

It seems crazy to me that a person has to work so hard for Social Security and Medicare programs and services that are provided to them under the law already. The big problem is that most people do not know what their rights are when it comes to receiving benefits. Anyone who has ever tried to read a lengthy, convoluted government regulation has often been left empty, frustrated, confused, or all of the above. I have to ask myself, why is this? I have found that often times, experts who are charged with providing information to the general public – governmental supervisors, politicians, legislators, case representatives, and educators – miss the mark over and over again. I do not imagine any of them have spent too much time in the proverbial "hot seat" as is the case with the numerous people I have interviewed.

When I was a reporter for a local newspaper, I had the opportunity to participate in occupational "ride-alongs."

What this meant was that every week or so I would spend a few hours, or even an entire day, with a chosen person in a particular field. Given that I had a background in military law-enforcement, I tended to gravitate toward observations with police officers, detectives, and other occupations of that sort. Unfortunately, there was often an annoying element of performance getting in the way of what I wanted to know. If I rode with cops, for example, I always got the anesthetized vision of what "cop-life" entailed – the "Hill Street Blues" version, if you will.

After I entered graduate school, I got into a kind of an angry political activist phase and started reading Abbie Hoffman books. I was not by any stretch of the imagination an outrageous 1960s political activist, but elements in his books did have an influence on me. A lot of his stuff had to do with the rights individuals had in their society to manage their own lives, free from undue influence from the federal government.

During my study, I volunteered to do a thesis that talked about how a system like the government might operate. I wanted to focus on something theoretical that no one else had tried before. My paper would focus on how, and in what way, unspoken forms of communication either promote or inhibit a person's ability to be successful at something. I thought about my previous experiences as a reporter and decided that I would need to observe people to see what I could learn, but it had to be different this time. I started visiting college campuses, shopping malls, police stations, government offices, and sometimes I even sat in crowds and recorded my observations – with pencil, paper, or tape recorder. Sometimes, I would bring my kids to blend into a crowd. I wanted to eliminate that annoying performance factor that I had so often experienced during those previously mentioned occupational snore sessions. I eventually completed my research paper. It was shortly afterward that I received the assignment to write this book. I decided to put the spy skills I acquired as a staff writer to work once again.

The goal of this handbook is a truly heartfelt attempt to provide the reader with the most useful information about Social Security and Medicare possible. When I say useful, I am not talking about a blanket of mindless, meaningless statistics. That has been done to death. I do not think that the everyday person responds well to complex or abstract figures and numbers – unless he or she is an accountant, of course. This is not to speak ill of accountants, but from what I have discovered about some of the Social Security and Medicare regulations, it can take a Ph.D. in economics to understand what all the rules mean. Most people I know are not accountants, nor are they Ph.D.s, and to that end, I will try to be as clear as I possibly can. Additionally, I want give the everyday people contextual information that can help them. I know figures and statistics are important, especially when money is involved. I am also well aware of how those statistics may intensely affect lives, but I want to say something straight away. People are more than statistics. It is because of this that I have incorporated some personal advice in this book – advice to serve as a vital tool against potential administrative apathy for those who might need it. That to me is the type of useful stuff I really want to supply.

The Setup

This book is structured in such a way that the reader has the opportunity to get clear information, which may directly apply to his or her specific needs. The Introduction: Why You Need This Book! is self-explanatory. It may not be relevant to an application process necessarily, but I hope the reader will go through it as I believe they need to arm themselves against poisonous misinformation. There are tips embedded into sections of the book that I hope will dispel certain myths and misgivings people have about Social Security and Medicare that often hurt their chances of receiving benefits. Navigating the stream of regulatory obstacles governing Social Security and Medicare will be difficult, to say the least. To achieve the most desired success, try to anticipate these obstacles as strategies in a chess game. The ability to anticipate an opponent's next move in this respect will prove vital for survival. Know there are rules to the benefits game, so do not let anyone suggest otherwise.

Where Can I Find the Information I Need?

At the beginning of both Chapters 1 and 10, I have written a brief history of Social Security and Medicare, where the programs came from, when they were initiated, and who was involved in developing certain services. I have written about the Social Security Act and what I believe people need to know about court rulings, regulations, and other current information that will help them. Additionally, I have also written about how people may be adversely affected by regulations developed decades ago and how the more archaic language of these rules are often biased and serve to marginalize and even obscure certain communities entirely. These sections are entitled "Bias or Not?" and will be placed just prior to the summaries at the end of each relevant chapter. Put more simply, I will talk about how and in what way some of the rules just do not apply!

Chapters 2 through 12 have the "meat" of information I believe people will be looking for the most. These chapters will talk about the programs and services that both Social Security and Medicare offer. In these sections, I have incorporated overviews on application processes, eligibility guides, schedules, and details about how cash benefits are calculated. In addition, I have included some blank application forms and useful Internet sites and other information. Some chapters will only detail information about the more familiar names of programs and services provided by Social Security. Under the headings "Services and Programs," the reader can expect information on the following benefits: retirement, disability, dependent, survivor, and supplemental security income. In the "Special Coverage Provisions" portion, I have noted some of the more unfamiliar services and will talk about any corresponding vocabulary necessary to navigate the vast ocean of commonly garbled governmental terminology. The section "Other Benefits" will have information about additional extras that are a little less familiar to the public than details already talked about in previous chapters. The reader will find there are sections comprised of information about hospitals and insurance, medical insurance, drug coverage, and prescriptions under Social Security. There will also be a section entitled "Special Veterans Benefits" and I will mention rules governing eligibility and other pertinent information. I will again also note some usable vocabulary, and how specific knowledge may prove to be instrumental in getting help.

Help — I Have Been Denied!

Chapter 8 has an overview of administrative information during the Social Security application process – who specifically reviews applications, what is involved on a caseworker's end, and how long people can expect to wait for benefits. This chapter, I believe, is particularly relevant to most as it contains advice about what a reader can do if he or she is ever denied benefits. I have written about what a Social Security administrator, for example, may be looking for to reject claims he or she knows is viable. It is quite surprising to find how many decisions are stamped "not favorable" simply because the person applying for benefits lacks evidence of his or her circumstances. It happens often, and there is a lengthy appeal process of which I have also written about in this section. It seems as if being denied happens often, so I hope the reader will review this portion of the handbook carefully.

Insights from the Professionals

In Chapter 9, I incorporated case studies from professionals (attorneys, university professors, and advocacy groups) who have many years of combined experience with Social Security. The reader will also gain some good insight about how other countries have fared with their Social Security reform. The studies include information about privatization in the United Kingdom, Australia, Sweden, and Chile. Also in this section, I have written about current controversies people often hear about in the news, but may not understand entirely. I have done my best to lift the veil of uncertainty. Further, I have incorporated several Internet resources at the end of the chapter. Lastly, I added some case studies and other additional research about decision-making processes in both personal and business settings. This information is relevant as it may help the reader better understand how people think and interact in a business setting. The Social Security Administration is a business environment. Other sections will overview why controversies about Social Security may be relevant to the reader now, and in the future.

Medicare and More

Chapter 10 will have a general overview of Medicare with a similar format to the earlier Social Security portion of the book. Incorporated are a brief history, some pertinent rules and regulations, and other applicable information. I will talk about the Original Medicare and Medicare Advantage Plans and will have a brief outline on each of their subordinate categories known as: Parts A, B, C, and D. I have written about: hospital insurance, hospice and home health care, medically necessary services and supplies, managed health care, co-pays and premiums, outpatient care, doctor services, and prescription coverage. I have also incorporated a lot of vocabulary here, as well.

CONCLUSION

The conclusion of the book will simply wrap up everything detailed in the previous chapters as concisely as possible. I may add bits here and there, but that is how this book is laid out. What I want people to remember is that the various Social Security and Medicare programs available are not supposed to strip people of their dignity. Many people have told me that is precisely how they often feel when they have to sometimes lie, beg, borrow, and steal to be afforded certain rights they have already under the law. The programs are there to help, if you know the rules of the game. Do not let anyone treat you as less than you deserve, so toward that end, let me tell you why you need this book.

INTRODUCTION: WHY YOU NEED THIS BOOK

I magine going into your local Social Security office with a pile of paperwork gathered in your hands. Walking by the "schnook" of a security guard in the lobby (whose eyes you feel burning into the back of your head as you pass), you enter into a room full of other people with similar paperwork. You grab a number and wait. Sitting silently, there seems to be enough tension left in the room to choke a small elephant from the loud argument that just emptied outside into the parking lot.

You are undaunted as you feel your case is solid, so you try not to notice the smelly guy with a baseball cap next to you with his finger up his nose. After about 45 minutes, someone calls out a number: "Number 12." Your number is 32. Finally, after what seems like an eternity, that same voice calls your number.

Approaching a silhouette through what appears to be a shroud of bulletproof glass, you shove your stack of information through the 12-by-4-inch opening and wait for a response. After the clerk takes up the mound of copies, he or she pulls up the case information taken during your previous visit on a computer monitor while you continue to stand in awkward silence. "This case has been closed," the clerk says. He or she then mercilessly pushes back your paperwork and tells you to kindly visit the office again when your information is complete. Stunned, you have no idea where to go from here.

Here is another one:

A working single mother has a baby who suffers constantly from undiagnosed and painful illnesses. The child grows and is unable, at more than two years old, to hear or even walk properly. The mother was neither an alcoholic nor a drug addict during her pregnancy, and she cannot imagine why her son is so intensely ill. The mother goes to the medical community for help. Doctors later say her son will need extensive medical care, but they cannot move forward with any prolonged treatment as she has no way to pay. She goes to the Social Security office for assistance. Time goes by, and the child sees numerous physicians, therapists, and specialists and gets the help he needs. The mother is given Supplemental Security Income compensation for the duration of the child's many surgeries and physical therapy appointments, old-style MRIs, and occupational-therapy sessions. Through some billing loophole in the system, Social Security tells the mother that an overpayment has been made to her and to those doctors, specialists, and therapists, and she is now required to pay it back or her case will be closed. The mother now owes Social Security thousands of dollars. She has no idea how something like this could have happened. When she was initially informed that her son was going to receive benefits, her case manager told her everything was fine. Having no knowledge of how the system works, and being unable to afford a lawyer's help, the mother's case is subsequently closed. Unable to get assistance anywhere else, she is left only to watch her child slowly deteriorate, year after year. She has no idea what to do.

Keep in Mind

The above two scenarios are compilations of real-life experiences designed to illustrate the sense of desperation that can result without adequate knowledge of the Social Security and Medicare systems. One primary way to avoid problems in the "just in case" arena is to know exactly what it is you are getting yourself into when applying for benefits. Have general knowledge about how the system works before you become a part of it. Be aware, however, that misinformation is a killer, so do not count on some overworked, underpaid Social Security case worker to know what it is you specifically need. This is not to suggest that all caseworkers and clerks are cold, callous, or all-out "bad." They just may not understand your needs, as every case and person may be different. Again, do not get me wrong; Social Security employees have a lot of knowledge about Social Security programs and services that you probably do not. Regrettably, however, I have had more than one personal experience with insensitive, even belligerent Social Security representatives. I did what most people do when they have a problem with a governmental employee, I asked for a supervisor. The representative then told me there was no one available. I asked for a supervisor's name, she said no names were available. I asked for her first and last name, she said her personal information was private. I tried calling on the telephone later that day and again, I had difficulty getting answers, so I asked for a supervisor. The person I was speaking to placed me on hold. After a good 25 minutes, a voice came on the phone and said, "If you would like to make a call, please hang up and dial again." A day or so later I went down to the same office, yet again, and sat inconspicuously in the back row for a brief period. I witnessed various incidents whereby Social Security Administration (SSA) representatives seemingly counted on a person's ignorance of the system. One old woman in particular was asking for help about paperwork concerning her dead husband. The SSA employees showed little compassion when this woman became so frustrated she was almost reduced to tears. I was angry about the treatment others and I had received. I kept asking myself, "What did I do wrong?" After some thought, I tried to consider approaching my future relationships with SSA employees in a new way.

The Lion and the Lamb

During both my undergraduate and graduate years in college, I had the opportunity to study a fair amount of philosophy. I remember a class discussion one day that had to do with a theory called "models of power and trust." The professor used an analogy about a lion and lamb to illustrate the potential struggle involved when others in real life have some kind of an unfair power and advantage over you – how some with that advantage may even inadvertently wield it, not knowing that they are doing it. The teacher said the circumstance may even be exacerbated when you become aware of your disadvantage and feel powerless to do anything. She said that feeling is common when hopelessness ensues and defeat is often the tool of your enemy. Let us say for the purpose of discussion that the type of advantage could be, for example, the power a caseworker has to approve or deny your benefit claim. You want something from him or her and he or she knows it. That is a form of advantage that many workers may unknowingly take for granted.

A major portion of the lion and lamb analogy talked about hunger. In the course of communicating with the other, that is, when the lamb said it was hungry, the lion was not affected in anyway. Because of the difference in power, the lion does not have to concern itself with whether or not the lamb is hungry, poor, or hopeless. Even if the lion were to try, it could never understand, because it has been a lion all of its life. The lion trusts the relationship is equal and it does not have to know anything about the lamb to survive. The twist in perspective comes in the story when the lamb has to worry whether or not the lion is hungry all the time. The lamb must always be aware of what the lion is feeling and thinking every minute of the affair – one slip and the lamb becomes dinner. The relationship is not equal even though the lion, through no fault of its own, might think it is.

To paraphrase, in any kind of relationship, the person with the most power essentially dictates how the relationship operates. The more powerful agent, in this case the lion, makes rules as to how the lamb will live and work. The lion sometimes makes rules to abide by, as well. He or she may even dole out consequences for particular lambs who do not comply. Each agent (lion or lamb) in this situation is not bound by the same set of rules, so measuring the other equally by the same standards is not practical, not helpful, and maybe even be just plain stupid. I am not trying to suggest that people who apply for benefits are lambs, nor am I suggesting that those who make determinations about cases are lions. After much review, it just seems to me as if the well-intended Social Security and Medicare system is a little broken.

I want you to learn how to be the lion and take back some real-life advantage. The next time that caseworker, clerk, or representative gives you information, possibly misinformation, about what to do with a claim, do not always take what he or she has to say as gospel. If you encounter difficulty, do not give up; get the facts first.

WHAT IS SOCIAL SECURITY?

HISTORY

From as far back as the 1800 B.C., societies have often had ways to assist citizens who are unable to support themselves financially. Some of the earliest documents in history talk about social aid for the elderly, the injured, sick, or infirmed, and they even mention ways to transfer estates to relatives of dead family members. Under the "poor laws" of 16th-century England, people who were injured on the job were given housing for the duration of their injuries until they were well again. Some were even given permanent housing in the event they were no longer able to work. Funding for the poor laws came from workers' taxes, and, in later day Europe, the laws became known as social welfare. Up until this era, there were no all-encompassing formal or publicly funded ways to help large portions of communities as a whole. The poor laws later transformed into more contemporary models of social insurance that were initiated by British settlers in 18th-century America. Most people during this period lived and worked on farms with their families for generations, or they were tradesmen of some sort. Those in need could often get help from worker-based organizations called "friendly orders" that are now referred to as "fraternal orders" from people within a similar trade – shoemakers for shoemakers, rock cutters for rock cutters, and builders for builders. After the Industrial Revolution, however, the need for a more overall formalized method of social support became necessary. These models became the basis for what people nowadays know as Social Security – a way to provide large-scale public provisions for the economic security and welfare of individuals and families in need.

The Townsend Club

In 1933, Francis Townsend, a formally trained physician and son of a farmer, was living in Long Beach, California, during the Great Depression when he lost his job as an assistant city health director. While walking down a city street, he saw three elderly women in an alley digging for food in garbage cans. Outraged by what he saw, he decided to become active in politics and started a group he called the "Townsend Club." In an effort to end the Great Depression, Townsend proposed that the federal government offer a pension to people over the age of 60.

Paid for by federal sales taxes, he proposed the Old Age Revolving Pension Plan (OARPP). By 1935, the Townsend Club had five million members and support for his OARPP grew to more than 20 million people nationwide. During this period, Townsend had generated some controversy over the issue and was labeled as a "crackpot." According to some historians, he walked up to President Franklin D. Roosevelt, who had created the Committee on Economic Security in 1934, and handed him a petition about the OARPP that had been supposedly signed by each one of those 20 million supporters. The idea that so many people had been unified so quickly sent Roosevelt, as well as other legislators of the period, into action. This petition resulted in Congress passing the Social Security Act the same year.

Mr. Townsend lived for another 25 years afterward. According to an October 2001 article from American Heritage Magazine, he lived just long enough to see the breadth of his vision realized:

"Not bad for a crackpot," Mr. Townsend said.

The Social Security Act

President Franklin D. Roosevelt started the Committee on Economic Security in 1934. He proposed a program guaranteeing that all U.S. citizens had some kind of social system of support. According to a report issued by the CPA Journal in May 2006:

President Roosevelt called for "social insurance." He envisioned a plan through which workers would contribute and provide for their own future economic security. He specifically disdained the idea of reliance upon welfare. The original SSA embraced the idea of Social Security being an insurance program under which a group of individuals were insured against identifiable risks: disability and old age. Workers paid for their own insurance. The concept pools the risk of disability or loss of income due to old age among a large number of individuals and pays out to those who live long enough to reap the benefit. If Social Security is thought of as an insurance program, then only those who had paid into the system should receive benefits. In addition, the benefit should be payable only to the insured individual and not to the insured's spouse or family. If the benefit can be paid to a spouse or family, then an individual without a spouse or family should be able to identify a "beneficiary." Finally, there should also be a direct correlation between the amount paid in and the benefit received, without a benefit cap or the taxation of benefits for wealthier recipients (CPA Journal 2006).

Reprinted from The CPA Journal, May, 2006, copyright 2006, with permission from the New York State Society of Certified Public Accountants.

In 1935, this committee imparted to Congress the Economic Security Bill, and Congress later changed the name to the Social Security Act. The bill was approved and signed into law in August of the same year, but not without controversy.

The Social Security Act is a compilation of laws that has 11 titles. Six are comprised of program names, while the others consist of rules regulating how the former programs are funded, and they have other information about creating public health facilities.

THE SOCIAL SECURITY ACT (ACT OF AUGUST 14, 1935) [H.R. 7260]
PREAMBLE

"An act to provide for the general welfare by establishing a system of Federal old-age benefits, and by enabling the several States to make more adequate provision for aged persons, blind persons, dependent and crippled children, maternal and child welfare, public health, and the administration of their unemployment compensation laws; to establish a Social Security Board; to raise revenue; and for other purposes. Be it enacted by the Senate and House of Representatives of the United States of America in Congress assembled..."

The Old Age Assistance and Benefits outlined specifics about retirement. Some of the other programs listed were called: Unemployment Compensation, Aid to Dependent

Children (ADC), Maternal and Child Welfare, and Aid to the Blind. Old Age Benefits (OAB) and Unemployment Compensation were considered the "social insurance" portion while the Old Age Assistance and Aid to the Blind were subcategories under the OAB. The Maternal and Child Welfare sections were made to help disabled and endangered children, poor mothers and their children, and any other homeless and neglected children. The ADC provided support for single-parent households comprised mainly of women or other relatives.

SOCIAL SECURITY ACT - TITLE I- GRANTS TO STATES FOR OLD-AGE ASSISTANCE

APPROPRIATION

SECTION 1. For the purpose of enabling each State to furnish financial assistance, as far as practicable under the conditions in such State, to aged needy individuals, there is hereby authorized to be appropriated for the fiscal year ended June 30, 1936, the sum of $49,750,000, and there is hereby authorized to be appropriated for each fiscal year thereafter a sum sufficient to carry out the purposes of this title. The sums made available under this section shall be used for making payments to States which have submitted, and had approved by the Social Security Board established by Title VII (hereinafter referred to as the Board), State plans for old-age assistance.

STATE OLD-AGE ASSISTANCE PLANS

SEC. 2.

(a) A State plan for old-age assistance must

(1) provide that it shall be in effect in all political subdivisions of

SOCIAL SECURITY ACT - TITLE I- GRANTS TO STATES FOR OLD-AGE ASSISTANCE

the State, and, if administered by them, be mandatory upon them;

(2) provide for financial participation by the State;

(3) either provide for the establishment or designation of a single State agency to administer the plan, or provide for the establishment or designation of a single State agency to supervise the administration of the plan;

(4) provide for granting to any individual, whose claim for old-age assistance is denied, an opportunity for a fair hearing before such State agency;

(5) provide such methods of administration (other than those relating to selection, tenure of office, and compensation of personnel) as are found by the Board to be necessary for the efficient operation of the plan;

(6) provide that the State agency will make such reports, in such form and containing such information, as the Board may from time to time require, and comply with such provisions as the Board may from time to time find necessary to assure the correctness and verification of such reports; and

(7) provide that, if the State or any of its political subdivisions collects from the estate of any recipient of old-age assistance any amount with respect to old-age assistance furnished him under the plan, one- half of the net amount so collected shall be promptly paid to the United States. Any payment so made shall be deposited in the Treasury to the credit of the appropriation for the purposes of this title.

SOCIAL SECURITY ACT - TITLE I- GRANTS TO STATES FOR OLD-AGE ASSISTANCE

(b) The Board shall approve any plan which fulfills the conditions specified in subsection (a), except that it shall not approve any plan which imposes, as a condition of eligibility for old-age assistance under the plan-

(1) An age requirement of more than sixty-five years, except that the plan may impose, effective until January 1, 1940, an age requirement of as much as seventy years; or

(2) Any residence requirement which excludes any resident of the State who has resided therein five years during the nine years immediately preceding the application for old-age assistance and has resided therein continuously for one year immediately preceding the application; or (3) Any citizenship requirement which excludes any citizen of the United States.

PAYMENT TO STATES

SEC. 3.

(a) From the sums appropriated therefor, the Secretary of the Treasury shall pay to each State which has an approved plan for old-age assistance, for each quarter, beginning with the quarter commencing July 1, 1935,

(1) an amount, which shall be used exclusively as old-age assistance, equal to assistance under the State plan with respect to each individual who at the time of such expenditure is sixty-five years of age or older and is not an inmate of a public institution, not counting so much of such expenditure with respect to any individual for any month as exceeds $30, and

SOCIAL SECURITY ACT - TITLE I- GRANTS TO STATES FOR OLD-AGE ASSISTANCE

(2) 5 per centum of such amount, which shall be used for paying the costs of administering the State plan or for old-age assistance, or both, and for no other purpose: Provided, That the State plan, in order to be approved by the Board, need not provide for financial participation before July 1, 1937, by the State, in the case of any State which the Board, upon application by the State and after reasonable notice and opportunity for hearing to the State, finds is prevented by its constitution from providing such financial participation.

(b) The method of computing and paying such amounts shall be as follows:

1) The Board shall, prior to the beginning of each quarter, estimate the amount to be paid to the State for such quarter under the provisions of clause (1) of subsection (a), such estimate to be based on

(A) a report filed by the State containing its estimate of the total sum to be expended in such quarter in accordance with the provisions of such clause, and stating the amount appropriated or made available by the State and its political subdivisions for such expenditures in such quarter, and if such amount is less than one-half of the total sum of such estimated expenditures, the source or sources from which the difference is expected to be derived,

(B) records showing the number of aged individuals in the State, and

SOCIAL SECURITY ACT - TITLE I- GRANTS TO STATES FOR OLD-AGE ASSISTANCE

(C) such other investigation as the Board may find necessary.

(2) The Board shall then certify to the Secretary of the Treasury the amount so estimated by the Board, reduced or increased, as the case may be, by any sum by which it finds that its estimate for any prior quarter was greater or less than the amount which should have been paid to the State under clause (1) of subsection (a) for such quarter, except to the extent that such sum has been applied to make the amount certified for any prior quarter greater or less than the amount estimated by the Board for such prior quarter.

(3) The Secretary of the Treasury shall thereupon, through the Division of Disbursement of the Treasury Department and prior to audit or settlement by the General Accounting Office, pay to the State, at the time or times fixed by the Board, the amount so certified, increased by 5 per centum.

(1) that the plan has been so changed as to impose any age, residence, or citizenship requirement prohibited by section 2 (b), or that in the administration of the plan any such prohibited requirement is imposed, with the knowledge of such State agency, in a substantial number of cases; or

(2) that in the administration of the plan there is a failure to comply substantially with any provision required by section 2 (a) to be included in the plan; the Board shall notify such State agency that further payments will not be made to the State until

SOCIAL SECURITY ACT - TITLE I- GRANTS TO STATES FOR OLD-AGE ASSISTANCE

the Board is satisfied that such prohibited requirement is no longer so imposed, and that there is no longer any such failure to comply. Until it is so satisfied it shall make no further certification to the Secretary of the Treasury with respect to such State.

OPERATION OF STATE PLANS

SEC. 4. In the case of any State plan for old-age assistance which has been approved by the Board, if the Board, after reasonable notice and opportunity for hearing to the State agency administering or supervising the administration of such plan, finds-

ADMINISTRATION

SEC. 5. There is hereby authorized to be appropriated for the fiscal year ending June 30, 1936, the sum of $250,000, for all necessary expenses of the Board in administering the provisions of this title.

DEFINITION

SEC. 6. When used in this title the term old age assistance means money payments to aged individuals."

It was during this period that control of these monies fell under the care of a governmental body called the Social Security Board, whose name was later changed to the Social Security Administration a few years after World War II.

SOCIAL SECURITY ACT OF 1935: TITLE VII- ESTABLISHMENT OF THE SOCIAL SECURITY BOARD

ESTABLISHMENT

SECTION 701. There is hereby established a Social Security Board (in this Act referred to as the Board) to be composed of three members to be appointed by the President, by and with the advice and consent of the Senate. During his term of membership on the Board, no member shall engage in any other business, vocation, or employment. Not more than two of the members of the Board shall be members of the same political party. Each member shall receive a salary at the rate of $10,000 a year and shall hold office for a term of six years, except that

(1) any member appointed to fill a vacancy occurring prior to the expiration of the term for which his predecessor was appointed, shall be appointed for the remainder of such term; and

(2) the terms of office of the members first taking office after the date of the enactment of this Act shall expire, as designated by the President at the time of appointment, one at the end of two years, one at the end of four years, and one at the end of six years, after the date of the enactment of this Act. The President shall designate one of the members as the chairman of the Board.

DUTIES OF THE SOCIAL SECURITY BOARD

SEC. 702. The Board shall perform the duties imposed upon it by this Act and shall also have the duty of studying and making recommendations as to the most effective methods of providing

SOCIAL SECURITY ACT OF 1935: TITLE VII– ESTABLISHMENT OF THE SOCIAL SECURITY BOARD

economic security through social insurance, and as to legislation and matters of administrative policy concerning old-age pensions, unemployment compensation, accident compensation, and related subjects.

EXPENSES OF THE BOARD

SEC. 703. The Board is authorized to appoint and fix the compensation of such officers and employees, and to make such expenditures, as may be necessary for carrying out its functions under this Act. Appointments of attorneys and experts may be made without regard to the civil-service laws.

REPORTS

SEC. 704. The Board shall make a full report to Congress, at the beginning of each regular session, of the administration of the functions with which it is charged.

Since its inception, the Social Security Act has been modified repeatedly. One of the first major changes came in 1939, when the government decided to add benefits for family members of both retired and deceased workers. Another major change came with President Dwight D. Eisenhower and Congress, who added monthly benefits for disabled workers in 1956. Two years after Kennedy's assassination in 1963, President Lyndon Johnson signed an amendment creating Medicare, a new program that provided hospital insurance to elderly citizens. Both programs have seen many changes since.

Opposition to the Social Security Act

The constitutionality of the Social Security Act came under fire soon after it was enacted. The 10th Amendment of the Constitution was designed to explicitly prohibit the federal government from having unlimited power. The "reserve clause" in the amendment says that power not specifically granted to the federal government by the Constitution fell under the control of the states and its people. Further, if the federal government ever sought to increase its power, it had to have a legal reason and it must justify those reasons to the people accordingly. The Social Security Act sought to expand federal government powers, its taxing powers that is, in a way that had never been tried before. The Supreme Court had previously shot down portions of President Roosevelt's New Deal in 1934 for this reason. Shortly thereafter, Roosevelt responded to this action by trying to expand his own power to mandate who in the Supreme Court was allowed to stay on the bench. Business owners expressed opposition and became more than a little concerned watching from the sidelines while the "powers that be" fought so feverishly among themselves. One case opposing the Social Security Act was brought about by the Steward Machine Company. The company demanded that the Unemployment Compensation portion of the Act was tantamount to federal coercion. Company officials said the federal government did not have the right to intervene by forcing companies to pay out unemployment money, as it was not for the "good" of the country. The Alabama-based company said it had already paid out portions of taxes to the government, and then demanded the money be paid back citing the unconstitutionality of the new law. Carmichael v. Southern Coal & Coke Company and Gulf States Paper was a case that not only sought to argue the validity of the law, but also questioned the power the government had to tax companies to the brink of extinction. Both companies brought their fight to the U.S. Supreme Court. The final legal fight during this period, brought about by Edison Electric Illuminating Company of Boston, Massachusetts, also carried the long-standing battle to the Supreme Court. In Helvering v. Davis, the Supreme Court decided the Social Security Act was constitutional. In May 1937, Justice Benjamin N. Cardozo delivered his opinion about the case to address the widespread oppositional concern:

> *The purge of nation-wide calamity that began in 1929 has taught us many lessons. Not the least is the solidarity of interests that may once have seemed to be divided. Unemployment spreads from state to state; the hinterland now settled that in pioneer days gave an avenue of escape. ... But the ill is all one or at least not greatly different whether men are thrown out of work because there is no longer work to do or because the disabilities of age make them incapable of doing it. Rescue becomes necessary irrespective of the cause. The*

hope behind this statute to save men and women from the rigors of the poor house as well as from the haunting fear that such a lot awaits them when journey's end is near.

Source: **www.multied.com/documents/Helvering.html**. Reprinted with permission of **http://www.historycentral. com**.

Did You Know?

The fight about how the federal government could influence its people has its roots dating back to when the Constitution was first drafted. More than 140 years before the Social Security Act was initiated, Alexander Hamilton and James Madison, two of the country's founding fathers, both vehemently argued about how much influence the federal government should have over its citizens and what control it could have over the economy. Hamilton thought the federal government could levy taxes or initiate other federal spending, as it deemed appropriate for the overall well-being of the people. This ideal is referred to as the "doctrine of implied powers." Madison disagreed. He thought the manner in which the federal government could spend money (or levy taxes) should be specifically delineated within the Constitution to protect the people against a government that sought to restrict the people's autonomy over their own daily lives. This premise is referred to as "strict construction."

The Constitution was eventually framed in the hope of marrying the two ideals together.

How Did the Social Security Act Get Money?

The U.S. government started issuing Social Security cards to all of its citizens in 1937. The numbers on the cards are a way that the government can keep track of a worker's earnings and any taxes on those earnings that fund Social Security programs and benefits. The government puts the money into a trust fund to run its programs and cover the cost of operating such systems. A portion of this money is called Social Security Tax. The Social Security Act details where these specific taxes will go and to what programs will get money. The tax was later called the Federal Insurance Contributions Act (FICA).

EXECUTIVE ORDER 9397
NUMBERING SYSTEM FOR FEDERAL ACCOUNTS
RELATING TO INDIVIDUAL PERSONS

"WHEREAS certain Federal agencies from time to time require in the administration of their activities a system of numerical identification of accounts of individual persons; and

WHEREAS some seventy million persons have heretofore been assigned account numbers pursuant to the

Social Security Act; and

WHEREAS a large percentage of Federal employees have already

EXECUTIVE ORDER 9397
NUMBERING SYSTEM FOR FEDERAL ACCOUNTS
RELATING TO INDIVIDUAL PERSONS

been assigned account numbers pursuant to the Social Security Act; and

WHEREAS it is desirable in the interest of economy and orderly administration that the Federal Government move towards the use of a single, unduplicated numerical identification system of accounts and avoid the unnecessary establishment of additional systems:

NOW, THEREFORE, by virtue of the authority vested in me as President of the United States, it is hereby ordered as follows:

1. Hereafter any Federal department, establishment, or agency shall, whenever the head thereof finds it advisable to establish a new system of permanent account numbers pertaining to individual persons, utilize exclusively the Social Security Act account numbers assigned pursuant to Title 26, section 402.502 of the 1940 Supplement to the Code of Federal Regulations* and pursuant to paragraph 2 of this order.

2. The Social Security Board shall provide for the assignment of an account number to each person who is required by any Federal agency to have such a number but who has not previously been assigned such number by the Board. The Board may accomplish this purpose by (a) assigning such numbers to individual persons, (b) assigning blocks of numbers to Federal agencies for reassignment to individual persons, or (c) making such other arrangements for the assignment of numbers as it may deem appropriate.

EXECUTIVE ORDER 9397
NUMBERING SYSTEM FOR FEDERAL ACCOUNTS
RELATING TO INDIVIDUAL PERSONS

3. The Social Security Board shall furnish, upon request of any Federal agency utilizing the numerical identification system of accounts provided for in this order, the account number pertaining to any person with whom such agency has an account or the name and other identifying data pertaining to any account number of any such person.

4. The Social Security Board and each Federal agency shall maintain the confidential character of information relating to individual persons obtained pursuant to the provisions of this order.

5. There shall be transferred to the Social Security Board, from time to time, such amounts as the Director of the Bureau of the Budget shall determine to be required for reimbursement by any Federal agency for the services rendered by the Board pursuant to the provisions of this order.

6. This order shall be published in the FEDERAL REGISTER."

FRANKLIN D ROOSEVELT - THE WHITE HOUSE,
November 22, 1943.
*26 CFR, Cum. Supp., 402.502.
End.

By the 1970s, there was more money being paid out in benefits than there was money coming into the system. Because of the recession, the value of the funds held within Social Security, that is, the money taxed from contributor earnings, was worth less than it was when first collected. Inflation also caused desire for a wider array of programs as well as the need to increase benefits. It was around this period that people became worried as to whether or not the Social Security system would go bankrupt over time. Because millions of dollars had been generated over decades, the system was not in any imminent danger. Legislators, however, needed to create serious reform to ensure the future success of Social Security.

Social Security Reform Act of 1983

The National Commission on Social Security Reform, otherwise known as the "Greenspan Commission" (after economist Alan Greenspan), decided to address concerns about the longevity of the Social Security system. Some say this was a bold initiative by President Ronald Reagan to save Social Security. Under the Social Security Act of 1983, this commission generated more money by increasing taxes on Social Security benefits. What this meant was the degree to which taxes would be levied would be contingent on how much money a person made in the course of one year. For example, for a person who made more than $25,000 per year, and for married couples who made more than $35,000 per year, the taxes on these income ranges would increase by one-half. Tax rates also increased for those who were self-employed. The commission knew that the Social

Security system would still be in danger even with the tax increases, because the ratio of the senior population to working adults would invariably rise. This meant that Social Security would be paying out more money in benefits than it would be collecting – a disastrous circumstance, to say the least. Unless the commission did something about this, the Social Security system could not survive. The commission wanted help with their long-term planning because by the year 2050 there would be approximately twice as many senior citizens then there were in 1975. They decided to raise the retirement age to 66. President Clinton, under the request of the commission, developed the Advisory Council on Social Security in 1994 to design a plan that could fix the solvency problem for the future, as well. This simply means they had to figure out how to come up with enough money to pay out benefits in the years to come. Another change came when the Advisory Council decided to give incentives for potential retirees. The gist of it was that the Social Security would give incentives to those senior citizens who wanted to put off their retirement by five more years. By encouraging them to stay in the workforce longer, they could receive more money when they retired and the system would have a larger trust fund reserve. The council also decided to supplement the Social Security system with funds from private investors. This would mean control of the Social Security system would fall to private ownership.

PRIVATIZATION OF SOCIAL SECURITY?

Privatization means "to transfer to private ownership an economic enterprise or public utility that has been under state ownership." With regard to Social Security, advocates of this idea say that private companies are more efficient in dealing with money than government agencies are. According to some, companies could generate a lot more money and increase the quality of services overall. Social Security would be operated just like a business, and businesses compete with other businesses to become successful. A governmental agency, like Social Security, has no competitors, so they have little reason to "check" themselves, unless something becomes a problem. With no competition, the business of Social Security becomes a private monopoly and there is danger in this premise, as well. Some opponents of privatization say monopolies incite corruption. Those who are against it say companies ultimately exist to make money for their shareholders. Proponents say the door to corruption swings both ways, as the private sector does not have a monopoly on corruption. Businesses most assuredly give preferential treatment to their customers, essentially those who spend the most money. The amount of Social Security benefits paid to people would work in concert with the size of their prolonged investment into the system. Companies would profit from the people's taxes, minorities and women would be marginalized, and in this circumstance, individuals would have less right to benefits than major investors. In this respect, humanity and social consciousness takes a back seat to efficiency and utility. Social Security ceases to work in accordance with the ideals to which it was originally intended – to help those who cannot help themselves.

Regulations, Decisions, and Other Relevant Rulings

Since the 1937 decision, there have been many amendments to the Social Security Act, a major one of which later took into consideration the rise in inflation. This determination was designed to help citizens maintain a certain standard of living. In 1972, the Cost of Living Adjustments (COLAs) were designed to increase benefits payments under this premise. Because of COLA, additional amendments were enacted to allow for the combination of programs and services to incorporate more assistance for disabled people, which had originally only been intended for the blind. This new program would later be given the name "Supplemental Security Income," or "SSI," and it would be controlled by the federal government until 1980. What was once known as the Social Security Administration now became a section of the U.S. Department of Health and Human Services, another federally controlled agency. New Social Security regulations, reforms, and other legislation were developed and abolished over the course of the next 16 years. Perpetual department shuffling and constant name changing also added to much confusion. One of the most controversial Social

Security programs came in 1996 under President Bill Clinton. He got rid of Aid to Families with Dependent Children (AFDC), formerly ADC, and started the Temporary Aid for Needy Families (TANF). As its name suggests, the new program placed restrictions on how long, and in what way, families could receive various forms of assistance. This "work for welfare" program caused a major upheaval across the country. While some applauded the president's attempt to facilitate nationwide self-sufficiency, recipients of the Social Security program said the change was intensely unjust as it made no provisions for people, some of whom were uneducated, illiterate, and elderly, trapped by the regulations that came from regulatory guidelines designed in earlier programs. These guidelines restricted their ability improve their circumstances by going to school, which would otherwise enable them to earn a decent wage. People felt as if the new program virtually resigned them and their families to a status of "working class poor" forever.

Civil Rights and Social Security

The Civil Rights Act of 1964 was another major turning point in Social Security history. The new law addressed the topic of employment discrimination. According to the law, the 5th and 14th Amendments to the U.S. Constitution restrict the rights of both the state and federal governments to discriminate. The Constitution does not say anything about what a private company can or cannot do, however. The Civil Rights Acts of 1866 and 1867 were the first legislation pieces in the law to address outright employment discrimination, but both left too much room for legal maneuvering by wealthy individuals to do as they wished. To fill the gaps, Title VII of the 1964 Act was written as follows:

> *Unlawful employment discrimination by public and private employers, labor organizations, training programs, and employment agencies based on race or color, religion, sex, and national origin. Retaliation I as also prohibited by Title VII against any person for opposing any practice forbidden by statute, or for making a charge, testifying, assisting, or participating in a proceeding under the statute (42 US Code Chapter 21).*

This law was amended more than two and a half decades later. The Civil Rights Act of 1991 granted victims of discrimination the right to a jury trial. It would also expand the amount of money plaintiffs could receive in the event of a successful judgment order. Additionally, the law also greatly reduced an employer's ability to discriminate out of business necessity, as was the case of Patterson v. McLean Credit Union.

Flemming v. Nestor

When someone pays taxes into the Social Security system, it could be said they expect a certain return – a certain promise, if you will. Can the government take away a person's right to receive services already paid for? Can the government legally change eligibility requirements, for example, thus excluding that person from receiving future benefits for which they may have already paid? The answer is "yes," and Congress has done so, time and time again.

In the 1960 Supreme Court case Flemming v. Nestor, a man was legally denied benefits after he paid into the Social Security system for more than 19 years. Additionally, he was already receiving benefits once his case was denied. A portion of a previous 1954 amendment to the Social Security Act made it illegal to give benefits to people who had, at some point, been deported, in this case, deported for being a member of the Communist Party. Mr. Nestor argued that when he decided to pay taxes into the system, the government had entered into a sort of "contract" with him. He felt it was unconstitutional that the government, having accepted his payments for so many years, could go back on their "promise of future benefits." The Supreme Court disagreed. Under the "Reservation of Power" portion of Section 1104 of the Social Security Act, Congress is allowed to "alter, amend, or repeal any provision of this Act" they deem appropriate. The Supreme Court further mandated that the right to Social Security benefits was not contractual, but conditional.

OTHER LEGISLATION

There have been many amendments to Social Security over many years. Below is a brief look at significant Social Security related legislation in descending order from 2005 to 1935:

2005 – The Real ID Act

2004 – The Intelligence Reform and Terrorism Prevention Act

2003 – The Basic Pilot Program Extension and Expansion Act

2002 – Supplemental Appropriations Act

2001 – DOT and Related Agencies Appropriations Act

2000 – Social Security Numbers Confidentiality Act

1999 – DOT and Related Agencies Appropriations Act

1998 – The Omnibus Consolidated and Emergency Supplemental Appropriations Act

1997 – Taxpayer Relief Act

1996 – Personal Responsibility and Work Opportunity Reconciliation Act

1994 – Social Security Independence and Program Improvements Act

1990 – Food and Agriculture Resources Act

1988 – Housing and Community Development Act

1984 – Deficit Reduction Act

OTHER LEGISLATION

1983 – The Social Security Amendments

1982 – Debt Consolidation Act

1981 – Social Security Benefits Act

1978 – Food Stamp Act

1976 – Tax Reform Act

1974 – Privacy Act

1970 – Bank Records and Foreign Transaction Act

1965 – Internal Revenue Amendments

1943 – Executive Order 9397

1935 – The Social Security Act

BIAS or Not?

In 1964, the United States government modified portions of Social Security law. In Title VI of the Civil Rights Act, the U.S. Government could not discriminate against any person because of their "race, color, or national origin." The phrase "civil rights" refers to rights afforded to citizens who live in a given boundary – in this case, the United States. This is interesting to those of whom the Civil Rights Act is directed because they were already technically considered U.S. citizens under the law. As citizens, they should have been protected under the same rights afforded to those of already protected status. Some people in minority communities view this as intensely biased because measuring a group of people against a community of already "accepted" status is, to say the least, problematic.

SUMMARY

Chapter 1 covers:

Social Security – A History: From as far back as 1800 B.C., societies have often had ways to assist citizens who are unable to support themselves financially.

The Townsend Club: Francis Townsend helped initiate the Social Security Act when he formed the Townsend Club.

The Social Security Act: The Social Security Act is a compilation of laws that was first enacted in 1935. President Franklin D. Roosevelt started the Committee on Economic Security in 1934. He proposed a program guaranteeing that all U.S. citizens had some kind of social system of support. This committee imparted to Congress the Economic Security Bill, and Congress later changed the name to the Social Security Act.

Opposition to the Social Security Act: The Social Security Act sought to expand federal government powers, its taxing powers that is, in a way that had never been tried before. After the Social Security Act was signed, business owners fought the new law in a court battle that went all the way to the U.S. Supreme Court.

How did the Act get its money?: The government uses Social Security numbers to keep track of all the taxable money a worker makes over the years.

Social Security Reform Act of 1983: The government created one of the first major reforms to ensure the longevity of the Social Security system. Under the Social Security Act of 1983, the Greenspan Commission generated more money by increasing taxes on Social Security benefits.

Privatization: Means "to transfer to private ownership an economic enterprise or public utility that has been under state ownership." With regard to Social Security, advocates of this idea say that private companies are more efficient in dealing with money than government agencies.

Civil Rights Act of 1964: The Civil Rights Act of 1964 was another major turning point Social Security history. The new law addressed the overall topic of employment discrimination. According to the law, the 5th and 14th Amendments to the U.S. Constitution restrict the rights of both the state and federal governments to discriminate.

RETIREMENT BENEFITS

SECTION I: PROGRAMS & SERVICES - WHAT ARE THEY?

According to the *Social Security Handbook*, you may be eligible for many programs. The trick is trying to determine what services apply to your needs and whether you qualify for those services in the first place. A more familiar program under Social Security is retirement benefits. The three types of retirement are: Full, Early, and Delayed. To qualify for Full retirement, a person must be between 65 and 67 years old. One interesting factor here is that a person may continue working given they are at least 67 years old. If so, any income earned after that time does not reduce benefits. Early retirement starts at age 62, but you will not get the same benefits as those who are at the full retirement age. This is because you will be receiving benefits for a longer period. Delayed retirement means a person who does not apply for retirement until the age of 67. In this circumstance, the benefits will be larger than in Full or Early for obvious reasons.

For those retirees who were self-employed and are below the retirement age, the SSA requires that you inform them as to whether or not you will continue working after you want to receive benefits. There are limitations as to how much income you can have to remain eligible for retirement benefits. Regulations for 2007 state a person below retirement age who was self-employed can receive up to $12,960 a year and still be eligible for Social Security Retirement. According to SSA current information, for "every $2 a person (who is below retirement age) earns past this amount, $1 is withheld from your full retirement benefits." Once this person reaches the retirement age, the money is adjusted accordingly. Currently, SSA says the amount is adjusted $1 for every $3 a person earns over $34,440. If you are at the retirement age, SSA says you can receive benefits even if you decide not to retire from your business.

What Is an Earnings Record?

An earnings record is a statement documenting all of the money a person has paid in taxes to the Social Security system. It also has a summary of the benefits for which one may be eligible when they are so inclined to apply.

The Social Security office sends these statements out annually, but they will send individuals statements upon request. Knowing how much money you will be getting in the future can be invaluable toward your long-term financial planning. This report can also help you fix any potential errors that may impinge your ability to apply to receive future benefits. For example, if your statement read that you had "0" children when you have five or six, this may present problems for you. Additionally, if the Social Security office reported that you are now "deceased," this may serve to be problematic. I am overstating here, just to get the point across. In all reality, there have been crazy situations like this, so make sure your statement information is correct.

Am I Eligible?

The government determines eligibility for the types of retirement benefits based on age, how many years you have worked, and how much money you have made. The handbook says that if you have been employed (either working for yourself or someone else), are 62 years of age or older, and have earned a certain amount of credits (under those guidelines), you are eligible. Credits are simply determined by your work record, which is also determined by how much money you have received in your lifetime. This only talks about how much money you have earned that is "on record." For example, in 2007, a person needs to have earned $1,000 to receive one credit. The regulations for retirement benefits say a person can receive a maximum of four credits per year. To have a family member insured, however, a person needs to have earned a minimum of 40 credits in all. Given those requirements, your family may be eligible for benefits, too. According to the current *Social Security Handbook*, the requirements for family benefits say you must:

- Have a spouse who is at least 62 years old.

- If that spouse is at least 62 years old and takes care of a child under 16 (or disabled).

- Have unmarried children under 18 years old.

- Have unmarried children between the ages of 18 and 19 who are full-time students.

- Have children, any age, who are disabled, provided their disability has been established before the age of 22.

- Have a former spouse who is unmarried and at least 62 years old that was married to you for at least 10 years.

What If I Do Not Qualify?

There is not much a person can do to receive retirement benefits if they do not qualify under regulation standards. For those who have not earned 40 credits, they cannot receive Social Security benefits until they reach this requirement. Until they do so, their family member may not be eligible for benefits either. If you find that you do not have the credit requirement, do not worry; there may be other services for which you qualify (see "Auxiliary Benefits").

What Are Special Payments?

If a person receives money earned before they applied for benefits, SSA will consider this money a "special payment." Special payments in most circumstances do not affect the amount of retirement benefits a person can receive. Let us say you retire, apply for benefits, and later receive those benefits. At some point in time, you receive a check in the mail. This income was generated from wages that were earned before you retired. That is just one example of a special payment type, but others include: severance or back pay, sales commissions, and sick pay. According to SSA, if you were self-employed before you retired, "any net income you receive after the first year you retired counts as a special payment."

SOCIAL SECURITY ACT OF 1935: TITLE II – FEDERAL OLD AGE BENEFITS

OLD-AGE RESERVE ACCOUNT

Section 201.

(a) There is hereby created an account in the Treasury of the United States to be known as the Old-Age Reserve Account hereinafter in this title called the Account. There is hereby authorized to be appropriated to the Account for each fiscal year, beginning with the fiscal year ending June 30, 1937, an amount sufficient as an

SOCIAL SECURITY ACT OF 1935: TITLE II – FEDERAL OLD AGE BENEFITS

annual premium to provide for the payments required under this title, such amount to be determined on a reserve basis in accordance with accepted actuarial principles, and based upon such tables of mortality as the Secretary of the Treasury shall from time to time adopt, and upon an interest rate of 3 per centum per annum compounded annually. The Secretary of the Treasury shall submit annually to the Bureau of the Budget an estimate of the appropriations to be made to the Account.

(b) It shall be the duty of the Secretary of the Treasury to invest such portion of the amounts credited to the Account as is not, in his judgment, required to meet current withdrawals. Such investment may be made only in interest-bearing obligations of the United States or in obligations guaranteed as to both principal and interest by the United States. For such purpose such obligations may be acquired .

(1) on original issue at par, or

(2) by purchase of outstanding obligations at the market price. The purposes for which obligations of the United States may be issued under the Second Liberty Bond Act, as amended, are hereby extended to authorize the issuance at par of special obligations exclusively to the Account. Such special obligations shall bear interest at the rate of 3 per centum per annum. Obligations other than such special obligations may be acquired for the Account only on such terms as to provide an investment yield of not less than 3 per centum per annum.

(c) Any obligations acquired by the Account (except special obligations issued exclusively to the Account) may be sold at the

SOCIAL SECURITY ACT OF 1935: TITLE II – FEDERAL OLD AGE BENEFITS

market price, and such special obligations may be redeemed at par plus accrued interest.

(d) Whenever the Board finds that any qualified individual has received wages with respect to regular employment after he attained the age of sixty-five, the old-age benefit payable to such individual shall be reduced, for each calendar month in any part of which such regular employment occurred, by an amount equal to one month's benefit. Such reduction shall be made, under regulations prescribed by the Board, by deductions from one or more payments of old-age benefit to such individual.

PAYMENTS UPON DEATH

SEC. 203.

(a) If any individual dies before attaining the age of sixty-five, there shall be paid to his estate an amount equal to 3 1/2 per centum of the total wages determined by the Board to have been paid to him, with respect to employment after December 31, 1936.

(b) If the Board finds that the correct amount of the old-age benefit payable to a qualified individual during his life under section 202 was less than 3 1/2 per centum of the total wages by which such old-age benefit was measurable, then there shall be paid to his estate a sum equal to the amount, if any, by which such 3 1/2 per centum exceeds the amount (whether more or less than the correct amount) paid to him during his life as old-age benefit.

(c) If the Board finds that the total amount paid to a qualified individual under an old-age benefit during his life was less than the correct

SOCIAL SECURITY ACT OF 1935: TITLE II – FEDERAL OLD AGE BENEFITS

amount to which he was entitled under section 202, and that the correct amount of such old-age benefit was 3 1/2 per centum or more of the total wages by which such old-age benefit was measurable, then there shall be paid to his estate a sum equal to the amount, if any, by which the correct amount of the old- age benefit exceeds the amount which was so paid to him during his life.

PAYMENTS TO AGED INDIVIDUALS NOT QUALIFIED FOR BENEFITS

SEC. 204.

(a) There shall be paid in a lump sum to any individual who, upon attaining the age of sixty-five, is not a qualified individual, an amount equal to 3 1/2 per centum of the total wages determined by the Board to have been paid to him, with respect to employment after December 31, 1936, and before he attained the age of sixty-five.

(b) After any individual becomes entitled to any payment under subsection (a), no other payment shall be made under this title in any manner measured by wages paid to him, except that any part of any payment under subsection (a) which is not paid to him before his death shall be paid to his estate.

AMOUNTS OF $500 OR LESS PAYABLE TO ESTATES

SEC. 205. If any amount payable to an estate under section 203 or 204 is $500 or less, such amount may, under regulations prescribed by the Board, be paid to the persons found by the Board to be entitled thereto under the law of the State in which the deceased was domiciled, without the necessity of compliance with the requirements of law with respect to the administration of such estate.

SOCIAL SECURITY ACT OF 1935: TITLE II – FEDERAL OLD AGE BENEFITS

OVERPAYMENTS DURING LIFE

SEC. 206. If the Board finds that the total amount paid to a qualified individual under an old-age benefit during his life was more than the correct amount to which he was entitled under section 202, and was 3 ½ per centum or more of the total wages by which such old-age benefit was measurable, then upon his death there shall be repaid to the United States by his estate the amount, if any, by which such total amount paid to him during his life exceeds whichever of the following is the greater: (1) Such 3 ½ per centum, or (2) the correct amount to which he was entitled under section 202.

METHOD OF MAKING PAYMENTS

SEC. 207. The Board shall from time to time certify to the Secretary of the Treasury the name and address of each person entitled to receive a payment under this title, the amount of such payment, and the time at which it should be made, and the Secretary of the Treasury through the Division of Disbursement of the Treasury Department, and prior to audit or settlement by the General Accounting Office, shall make payment in accordance with the certification by the Board.

ASSIGNMENT

SEC. 208. The right of any person to any future payment under this title shall not be transferable or assignable, at law or in equity, and none of the moneys paid or payable or rights existing under this title shall be subject to execution, levy, attachment, garnishment, or other legal process, or to the operation of any bankruptcy or insolvency law.

SOCIAL SECURITY ACT OF 1935: TITLE II – FEDERAL OLD AGE BENEFITS

PENALTIES

SEC. 209. Whoever in any application for any payment under this title makes any false statement as to any material fact, knowing such statement to be false, shall be fined not more than $1,000 or imprisoned for not more than one year, or both.

DEFINITIONS

SEC. 210. When used in this title-- (a) The term "wages" means all remuneration for employment, including the cash value of all remuneration paid in any medium other than cash; except that such term shall not include that part of the remuneration which, after remuneration equal to $3,000 has been paid to an individual by an employer with respect to employment during any calendar year, is paid to such individual by such employer with respect to employment during such calendar year. (b) The term "employment" means any service, of whatever nature, performed within the United States by an employee for his employer, except- (1) Agricultural labor; (2) Domestic service in a private home; (3) Casual labor not in the course of the employer's trade or business; (4) Service performed as an officer or member of the crew of a vessel documented under the laws of the United States or of any foreign country; (5) Service performed in the employ of the United States Government or of an instrumentality of the United States; (6) Service performed in the employ of a State, a political subdivision thereof, or an instrumentality of one or more States or political subdivisions; (7) Service performed in the employ of a corporation, community chest, fund, or foundation, organized and operated exclusively for religious, charitable, scientific, literary,

SOCIAL SECURITY ACT OF 1935: TITLE II – FEDERAL OLD AGE BENEFITS

or educational purposes, or for the prevention of cruelty to children or animals, no part of the net earnings of which inures to the benefit of any private shareholder or individual. (c) The term "qualified individual" means any individual with respect to whom it appears to the satisfaction of the Board that- (1) He is at least sixty-five years of age; and (2) The total amount of wages paid to him, with respect to employment after December 31, 1936, and before he attained the age of sixty-five, was not less than $2,000; and (3) Wages were paid to him, with respect to employment on some five days after December 31, 1936, and before he attained the age of sixty-five, each day being in a different calendar year."

SECTION II: APPLYING FOR BENEFITS

How Do I File a Claim?

Before applying for benefits, a person needs to know what he or she hopes to accomplish in doing so – primarily, people do it for the money. The application process is just a way for Social Security to know what is on your mind, so you might want to know what that is before you expect others to help. After that, get an application and fill it out. The online version of the *Social Security Handbook* says the best time to start your application is four months before you hope to receive benefits. Of course, do not wait until your situation is dire before you decide to do anything about it, as well. For disability, Social Security suggests you file one month before you want to receive benefits. This is to establish something called the "period of disability" within the system. One should apply for survivor benefits, however, as soon as possible. Discussion about Disability and Survivor Benefits is detailed in later chapters. Below is a list of documents needed to get an application going as well as information about where to send your application once it is completed:

- Social Security number

- Birth certificate

- W-2s or self-employment tax forms

- Discharge papers from the military (if it applies)

- Spouse's Social Security number & birth certificate (if applying for them)

- Children's Social Security number & birth certificates (if applying for them)

- If not born in the United States, provide proof of citizenship

- Bank account information (if you want to use direct deposit)

A person also has the option of applying for benefits online, and most people say this is the best way to expedite matters. For an online application, go to: **http://www. socialsecurity.gov**. If you want to file in person, you may go to your local Social Security office. According to Social Security regulations, an application is consider filed when a person or office of authority "receives it." Sometimes the Social Security office will change the date on an application provided there are mitigating circumstances. For example, if a person wanted to establish an earlier filing date, for whatever reason, their application should be in an envelope with a valid postmark. A person will also get extra consideration changing an application date if they are either in the Armed Services overseas or active parts of Foreign Service.

How Much Money Can I Get?

The amount of money a person can get is determined by lifetime earnings, so each amount can vary. Social Security determines the amount by averaging your earnings in a period of your life in which you earned the most. People statistically earn the most money during a specific portion of their lives. For example, someone who starts work as a teenager would not typically make more money then they would as a 28-year-old adult. Social Security then calculates your monthly earnings and adjusts your monies accordingly each year they are received. They also consider changes in your average salary and adjust that as well. Social Security then applies a predetermined formula, or primary insurance amount (PIA), to figure your projected benefit amount. This amount is how much you will receive at your Full retirement age between 65 and 67 years old.

Earning Record Worksheet

According to the Social Security Web site, you can get a helpful worksheet from Social Security that will assist you in figuring out the numbers for yourself. Many people find the paperwork complicated, so keep in mind that your results may vary. For example, once you get the worksheet, you will notice a list of years in the left-most column. Look for the years that apply to you and then enter the dollar amount of your earnings record in Column B. Know that this number should not be more than the previous column (Maximum Earnings). If you have not earned anything, enter the number "0." Next, multiply the dollar amounts of Column B and Column C. This will give you what the government refers to as "indexed earnings." Third, after you have figured out your complete tally, pick from Column D the 35 years in which you earned the most money. This means you add up the years, in a 35-year span, when you earned the most. Fourth, after you get your sum, divide by 420, because there are 420 months in 35 years. This part is divided into three subcategories: a) Round down to the next dollar amount and then multiply the first $680 (of those 35 years) by 90 percent (.9), b) Take that amount and multiple it over $680 dollars less than or equal to $4,100 by 32 percent (.32), c) take the amount you got after the fourth step, that is meaning the number you found after previously divided by 420. Take that dollar amount and multiply it over $4,100 by 15 percent (.15). Now add the sums of everything you determined for parts a, b, and c.

This will illustrate the full retirement benefits you may receive, if you meet the overall general requirements. Take that number and multiply by 75 percent (.75). This will give an estimate on what a person can receive at Early Retirement. Remember, these formulas will only give you estimates about what you may receive.

More About PIAs

Let us back up for a minute because that last section may have been a little confusing. The topic of primary insurance amounts (PIAs) is confusing for some, so according to the Social Security Administration (SSA) Web site, PIAs are the benefits a person receives if they retire at the "normal" retirement age. The SSA calculates this by averaging the dollar amount of money a person makes over a predetermined set of years. Typically the SSA will only look at the 35 years in which you made the most money. This average is referred to as "indexed monthly earnings." According to the SSA, the PIA formula from the last section goes as follows for people in 2008:

> *For people who become eligible for benefits, the PIA will be the sum of 90 percent of the first $711 of a person's average monthly index, plus 32 percent of the average indexed monthly earning over $711 up to $4,288, plus 15 percent of a person's average monthly index*

monthly earning over $4,288. We round this amount to the next lower multiple of $.10.

What Do Tax Reports Have to Do with Anything?

The Social Security Administration needs to ensure your tax information is correct before you become eligible for benefits. To make sure you qualify for a given amount of credits and benefits, the SSA needs to know the dollar amount of taxes a person has paid into the Social Security system over the duration of their employment lifetime. This is to prevent things like fraud, but it is also to protect potential beneficiaries. Both employees and employers have tax information that identifies them to the SSA. Sometimes having your tax report will enable Social Security to identify portions of your income that may or may not be taxable at all. Those who were self-employed may be eligible for additional benefits provided their tax reports are complete and accurate. According to the SSA, the government takes additional consideration when determining work credits (determined by info in their tax reports) for women who have to leave their employment to care for children or parents. They typically have fewer years in the work force, so the SSA may adjust potential benefits with this in mind. Again, this is if they meet certain legal criteria.

SECTION III: AUXILIARY BENEFITS

What Are Auxiliary Benefits?

By definition the term "auxiliary" means something "acting in support or supplement." Auxiliary Benefits is the name of the extra benefits that support, or even further, the primary benefits programs and services available under Social Security. Every program under Social Security has some form of added benefits, but the Auxiliary Benefits programs apply to retirement, disability, or survivor cases. These types of benefits are paid out to family members of a qualifying primary account holder. These benefits are also paid to family members based on the earnings record of the person who has paid Social Security taxes.

Who Is Eligible?

Family members can receive these benefits only if the primary holder has earned a predetermined amount of money. This is calculated by their Earnings Record, once again. The amount of money one can receive ranges from about 150 percent of the primary account holder's primary insurance amount (PIA). If the primary account holder has more than one child on his or her earnings record, for example, that PIA percentage could be a little more. In most circumstances, a person cannot receive the full amount of all three types of benefits at once. Any benefits a person does receive are adjusted yearly according to the Consumer Price Index (CPI). This index is a way of measuring the average cost of goods and services a typical household may buy.

SUMMARY

Chapter 2 covers:

Retirement benefits: This section covers what retirement benefits are, who qualifies, and what to look for during the application processes. This portion talks about how benefits are calculated, and what to do if you do not initially qualify.

Applying for benefits: This section talks about what to do when you want to apply for retirement benefits – how to file a claim and what money a person can expect to receive if approved. It also talks about Earning Record Worksheets, tax reports, and PIAs.

Auxiliary benefits: Refers to any benefit program that acts in support of another.

Who is eligible?: Family members can receive these benefits only if the primary holder has earned a predetermined amount of money. This is calculated by his or her Earnings Record, once again. The amount of money one can receive ranges from about 150 percent of the primary account holder's primary insurance amount (PIA).

What is an Earnings Record?: An earnings record is a statement documenting all of the money a person has paid in taxes to the Social Security system. It also has a summary of the benefits for which one may be eligible if he or she is so inclined to apply. The Social Security office sends these statements out annually, but they will send individuals statements upon request. Knowing how much money you will be getting in the future can prove to be invaluable toward your long-term financial planning.

Am I eligible?: The government determines eligibility for the types of retirement benefits based on age, how many years you have worked, and how much money you have made. The handbook says that if you have been employed (either working for yourself or someone else), are 62 years of age or older, and have earned a certain amount of credits (under those guidelines), you are eligible. Credits are determined by your work record, which is also determined by how much money you have received in your lifetime.

What are Special Payments?: If a person receives money earned before he or she applied for benefits, SSA will consider this money a "special payment." Special payments in most circumstances do not affect the amount of retirement benefits a person can receive.

File a claim: Get an application and fill it out. You can do this online or by filling out one at your local SSA office. The best time to start your application is about four months before you hope to receive benefits.

"Knowing others is intelligence; knowing yourself is true wisdom. Mastering others is strength; mastering yourself is true power."

DISABILITY BENEFITS

SECTION I: PROGRAMS & SERVICES – WHAT ARE THEY?

According to the *Social Security Handbook*, you may be eligible for many programs. The trick is trying to determine what services apply to your needs and whether you qualify for those services in the first place. A more familiar program under Social Security is retirement benefits. The three types of retirement are: Full, Early, and Delayed. To qualify for Full retirement, a person must be between 65 and 67 years old. One interesting factor here is that a person may continue working given they are at least 67 years old. If so, any income earned after that time does not reduce benefits. Early retirement starts at age 62, but you will not get the same benefits as those who are at the full retirement age. This is because you will be receiving benefits for a longer period. Delayed retirement means a person who does not apply for retirement until the age of 67. In this circumstance, the benefits will be larger than in Full or Early for obvious reasons.

WHAT IS A DISABILITY?

According to the Social Security Act, the term "disability" is defined for an adult as the "inability to engage in any substantial gainful activity by reason of any medically determinable physical or mental impairment which can be expected to result in death or has lasted or can be expected to last for a continuous period of not less than 12 months." A medically determinable impairment can be evaluated by "medically acceptable clinical or laboratory diagnostic techniques." This means if you cannot go back to work, any work, for an extended period because of a physical or mental problem, you can receive benefits. This does not mean you need to have been sick for more than a year, but the Social Security Administration (SSA) considers your illness as a potential impairment when you have not, or will not, have recovered after about three months. Also, to be disabled does not necessarily mean you have been forever resigned to a wheelchair or a similar situation. It also does not mean, although it could, that you have to be so sick that you may soon die.

WHO IS ELIGIBLE FOR BENEFITS?

The SSA has what they call a "five-step evaluation process"

to figure if you are technically considered disabled. First, the SSA will want to know if you are working. If you are, it does not mean you automatically do not qualify. The rules say a person can be considered disabled if they work; they just cannot earn more than, for 2007, $900 a month. The benefits are slightly increased for blind people. Secondly, they will want to know if your illness is serious. If you have trouble walking, sitting, or remember things, the SSA will consider you disabled. Thirdly, a rep will see if your illness is listed on what the SSA office terms as a "List of Impairments." The list is pretty long, but any neurological (like epilepsy, for example), psychological (this would include mental retardation), or physiological ailments will be included. Fourthly, to be considered disabled, a person cannot be able to go back to the same type of job he or she had previously. Let us say a person is a block mason, for example, and he or she has a debilitating arthritis condition that is going to prevent him or her from being able to build houses for a long time. This may mean he or she can be defined as "disabled." Lastly, the SSA will want to know if a person can get a job doing something else. They will consider your age, education, and other work background. If your sickness or impairment stops you from being able to get another job, you may qualify as disabled under this fifth step in the evaluation process. If you have lost a job and can prove the loss was caused directly because of your disability or illness, be sure to make a note about how the sickness or disability affected your ability to work. Try to get verification of this from a doctor.

The definition of disability is the same for children, with the only marked difference being that a child's impairment must "cause severe functional limitation." This means the limitation seriously inhibits a child's development or activity. A child also cannot earn more than $900 a month. If your child does make more than $900 a month, the SSA will not consider your child disabled. Additionally, the illness has to be expected to last for more than a year. The SSA Web site has a list of basic requirements they look at when considering whether your child falls within the definition. According to the *Social Security Handbook*, you have to prove your child's disability, too. The SSA will require detailed information from any doctors, specialists, or other professionals be sent to their offices. If for some reason a child has not yet been evaluated, they will let you know how to proceed from there. But you must ask; do not simply leave an office believing your child cannot get any help. Many people who try to get disability for their children do not have the means to pay for doctors or specialists. Also, having to care for a disabled child seriously impinges on a parent's ability to earn money, and the SSA office will consider this. SSA workers are a lot more compassionate regarding cases involving disabled children.

According to *Nolo's Guide to Social Security Disability*, if you think you are impaired, apply. The guide says that "older people, meaning 50 years of age or older, need not have as severe impairment as someone under 50." People will need a doctor's determination to figure out how long their sickness or impairment may last. This is important. The duration of disability, as determined by a physician, may have a lot to do with how much money a person can get and for how long. Additionally, the Social Security Administration has a set of guidelines detailing who is eligible for what types of benefits. Remember, age is not a sole factor. Any person can apply.

WHAT ABOUT MY FAMILY?

The guidelines for determining whether family members can get disability benefits are similar to the ones for retirement benefits. (For more information, see Retirement Benefits, "Am I eligible?"). Under disability benefits, the SSA may consider a former spouse eligible for benefits, even if he or she was not married to you for more than ten years. Also, the benefits paid to this former spouse will not necessarily reduce the amount you get for your current spouse or children. If for some reason you have government benefits, the amount you can receive from disability may be affected.

TYPES OF DISABILITY BENEFITS

Social Security Disability Insurance

There are two types of benefits programs: Social Security Disability Insurance (SSDI) and Supplemental Security Income (SSI). Social Security disability is the program that gives benefits to adults who are impaired because of a medical condition. This condition should be anticipated to last for a lengthy period, and the income requirement range is more than for SSI. To qualify for Social Security disability benefits, you have to pass two portions of something called "an earnings test." The first portion, the "recent work test," considers your age at the time you became disabled. The second part, the "duration of work test," determines whether or not you worked long enough in the system.

Rules for the recent work test state that if a person becomes disabled on or around their 24th birthday, the person is required to have "1.5 years of work during the three-year period ending with quarter your disability began." This means you need to have been working for at least half the time during the three years before you became disabled. The same rule says that if someone became disabled after his or her 24th birthday, but before his or her 31st birthday, they would need to have worked for at least three years over a six-year work period. The last of the "recent work test" requires that if the disability occurred after a person's 31st birthday, he or she would need to have worked for five years out of a ten-year work period before their disability began. According to the handbook, the "duration of work test" does not require that the work history fall within a given portion of time. This section simply says if you become disabled before you are 28 years old, you need 1.5 years of work to receive Social Security disability. As you get older, the work requirement for this program increases. At 38, the work requirement is four years and by age 60, you have to have worked for at least 9.5 years to qualify.

Supplemental Security Income

The Supplemental Security Income (SSI) program gives benefits to the blind, people who are age 65 or older, or people who have a disability. The SSA manages this program, and it is paid for by U.S. Treasury general funds. President Richard Nixon implemented the program in 1972, and it started two years afterward. The system suffered severe cutbacks after the 1980s, and therefore many states now add their own money in grants to the keep the program running.

To qualify for SSI you have to be living the United States and be a citizen. There was some initial debate about non-citizens getting benefits in the 1980s and 90s. Fueled by anti-welfare sentiment, major funding was slashed during this period because SSI sometimes paid benefits to people who were alcoholics and drug addicts – a form of disability under the law. Further cutbacks came about in 1996, when the law was re-drafted to exclude benefits paid to legal aliens. These reforms were considered by some as overly cruel because many legal aliens did not have the means to self-sustain, and many could not get jobs that paid more than minimum wage.

HOW IS ELIGIBILITY DETERMINED?

The people who qualify for this program have to be of limited income and resources. The SSA considers income as money you earn from working or wages. They also consider income defined as any Social

Security benefits and pensions you may get. The state you live in may also have an effect on your eligibility. If you are married and your spouse earns money, this may have an effect. Eligibility status will vary tremendously depending on how serious a disability is and who is disabled. The SSA defines "resources" as things like bank accounts, real estate, and stocks or bonds. Given this, a person may still be eligible even if they have these resources, but these resources cannot amount to more than $2,000. According to the Social Security Information Web site, a couple may not have resources of more than $3,000 to qualify. The site also states that if you own property and try to sell it, you may receive benefits while you do so.

The SSA does not discount a person simply because he or she has too many resources. They do not count the home you live in or the value of the land it is on when considering whether or not you may qualify. Additionally, you can own an inexpensive car, a burial plot, life insurance, or other types of funds that are each valued at about $1,500. There are other rules that the SSA considers when determining eligibility, some of which include such things as if you have already been approved for other Social Security benefits, and whether you live in an institution or shelter, rest home, or halfway house.

GENERAL DISABILITY REPORT FORM: (SSA-3368)

SOCIAL SECURITY ADMINISTRATION

Form Approved
OMB No. 0960-0579

**DISABILITY REPORT
ADULT**

For SSA Use Only
Do not write in this box.

Related SSN _____

Number Holder _____

SECTION 1- INFORMATION ABOUT THE DISABLED PERSON

A. **NAME** *(First, Middle Initial, Last)*

B. **SOCIAL SECURITY NUMBER**

C. **DAYTIME TELEPHONE NUMBER** *(If you have no number where you can be reached, give us a daytime number where we can leave a message for you.)*

_____ _____ ☐ Your Number   ☐ Message Number   ☐ None
Area Code   Number

D. Give the name of a **friend or relative** that we can contact (other than your doctors) **who knows about your illnesses, injuries or conditions** and can help you with your claim.

NAME _____   RELATIONSHIP _____

ADDRESS _____
(Number, Street, Apt. No.(If any), P.O. Box, or Rural Route)

_____   **DAYTIME** _____ _____
City   State   ZIP   **PHONE**   Area Code   Number

E. What is your **height** without shoes? ____ ____
feet   inches

F. What is your **weight** without shoes? _____
pounds

G. Do you have a **medical assistance card**? (For Example, Medicaid or Medi-Cal) If "YES," show the **number** here: ☐ YES ☐ NO
_____

H. Can you **speak and understand English**? ☐ YES ☐ NO   If "**NO**," what is your preferred language?_____

NOTE: If you cannot speak and understand English, we will provide an interpreter, free of charge.

If you cannot **speak and understand English**, is there someone we may contact who speaks and understands English and will give you messages? ☐ YES ☐ NO   *(If "YES," and that person is the same as in "D" above show "SAME" here. If not, complete the following information.)*

NAME _____   RELATIONSHIP _____

ADDRESS _____
(Number, Street, Apt. No.(If any), P.O. Box, or Rural Route)

_____   **DAYTIME** _____ _____
City   State   ZIP   **PHONE**   Area Code   Number

I. Can you **read and understand English**? ☐ YES ☐ NO

J. Can you **write more than your name in English**? ☐ YES ☐ NO

FORM **SSA-3368-BK** (2-2004) EF (2-2004) Use 6-2003 edition Until Supply Exhausted

PAGE 1

Disability Report-Adult-Form SSA-3368-BK

For the rest of this form, visit **http://www.ssa.gov/online/ssa-3368.pdf.**

PRESUMPTION OF DISABILITY

When you first apply, know that any person may be eligible to receive benefits during an initial application process. This is called "presumptive disability." This applies to people who are seeking SSI benefits only. A major determining factor is whether a person falls under the definition of disability noted earlier in this section. If so, the SSA will assume that if a person meets the definition, then in all likelihood, his or her application will be approved. You might also qualify for "emergency payments" if you can prove your circumstances are dire. An emergency payment is a one-time advance given to certain people (who apply for benefits in the first place) who are in immediate danger of some kind. This typically means there must be imminent danger to your health and safety. To get SSI initially, remember that a person must have a low income and have limited resources. To be considered eligible for presumptive disability, a person must apply for it. The SSA office says you are eligible if it is "reasonable" to consider you are disabled. If you have an obvious disability you will probably qualify – for example, if you have one or both of your arms or legs missing. Another immediate qualifier is if you are totally blind or deaf. Other less obvious disabilities can qualify for presumptive benefits, as well, but a person will need a reliable source to confirm it. If you have an HIV infection, for example, having medical confirmation about it is the best way to go – a doctor's note, if you will. The SSA determines presumptive requests in three ways: if you say you are disabled via a written statement, if the rep believes you, and if you have some kind of third party verification of your disability. If the SSA decides you are not eligible for presumptive benefits, the Disability Determination Service (DDS) may re-review your case. They approve presumptive benefits if you are mentally retarded, have a breathing disorder, have cancer or HIV infection, or if you have some kind of neurological disease that causes paralysis.

Conditional Benefits

If you are not eligible for presumptive or other benefits under SSI, you may qualify to get a loan from the SSA. Let us say you have real estate or investments of some kind that disqualify you. If you applied for SSI, for example, too many resources can cause a problem. The problem for you in this circumstance is that you are not able to get your hands on the cash you need right away. The SSA considers this. According to them, you need time to convert those assets to cash. It is during this period when you can qualify for "conditional benefits." Again, any money you receive must be paid back in full.

HOW DO I APPLY?

When applying for general disability benefits, using a telephone is a convenient way to file. A person can call the Social Security Administration at 1-800-772-1213. This is a good idea if you live a great distance from your local field offices. The SSA also has informative Web sites (at **www.socialsecurity.gov** or **www.ssa.gov**) where you can download many forms you will need to get an application started. If you do not have access to a computer, there are computers at your local public library. They may charge you a minimum to print forms, but the cost is minuscule. This may be your best way to get started if transportation is an issue. For those without cars and limited resources, know that your local job office has computers and fax machines for "job search" use. They will probably have you sign in at a front desk. No one will bother you, and there is no need to broadcast why you are there. If you live near a college, also know there are many computers for use at universities and community colleges. They have large libraries and computer labs of their own. They do not like to publicize this. The community colleges sometimes do not charge for printing forms out provided you are not trying to print out "book size" materials. The larger schools do not keep track of who goes in and out of their libraries. They have vast amounts of resources. My college campus alone had more than 45,000 students in attendance.

Typically, a disability examiner (with a doctor) makes the determination what will ultimately happen to a person's application. As if the case in with all Social Security applications, a person applying for SSI will need to have information from several sources. The SSA requires a Social Security card, birth certificate, payroll slips and bankbooks, a lease (if applicable), any medical information, and other proof of citizenship.

Make sure if you give them original documentation; the SSA representative makes copies. If for some reason you cannot get originals, the SSA will accept copies, but they have to be certified by someone they deem appropriate, such as a state agency. There are some circumstances when people cannot obtain an original copy of their birth certificate, and in this case the SSA may accept alternative documentation. The information has to have been recorded before the age of five years old. School or census records might be acceptable, as might insurance polices. In some cases, an SSA rep may even accept a signed statement from a doctor (otherwise referred to by SSA as a "treat source") or midwife who were present at your birth. The office also requires, again if applicable, information about where you live. They need a property owner's name, mortgage, or proof of a lease. Also, list all the names of medications you may be taking, and bring that list to the Social Security office. The best way to expedite your application is to make sure you have all the required paper work with you when initially applying. Do not wait until the day of an appointment, for example, to find some of the required information is missing. Understand the application process may take up to six months. This is not to say it will, but anything you can do to facilitate the process will help. Know that if you do get benefits, in some circumstances, the SSA may give you money retroactively. They will backdate your money. Let us say you started an application for disability benefits in March. It could take six months to get approval. Once approved in September, you are eligible to receive all the money for the period of time you had to wait over the course of those months. Know that if you are approved for either SSDI or SSI your dependents may also qualify for benefits.

WHAT ABOUT MY CHILD?

According to the SSA, children are eligible for SSI benefits if they are either blind or disabled. The SSA determines eligibility much like they do for the Social Security benefits program. The child has to have "marked and severe functional limitations" that inhibit or even paralyze their normal development. The disability has to be anticipated to last more than 12 months, as well. Additionally, the child should not be married or the head of a household. If your circumstances for some reason are dire, you should apply right away.

What Do I Have to Pay Back?

Once a case is approved, you will start to receive benefits soon thereafter, but be careful as the Social Security Administration oftentimes makes mistakes. Cases get mixed and mismatched, and dollars are sometimes sent to people who should not be receiving money. In some situations, the SSA can overestimate the amount of income you will receive over a given period. Sometimes a person can receive more benefits than those for which they are entitled. The SSA calls this difference between what is due and what is received "overpayment." If your case is approved and you receive benefits, make sure you know how much you will be receiving. Make sure the representative checks your information to ensure the numbers are correct. He or she will not like you questioning him or her, but ask the representative to do it nonetheless. Do not let him or her blow you off. If you do receive an overpayment, do not just pass it off either. Do not ignore it, as you will be responsible for paying back every penny. Simply viewing an overpayment as a "turn of good luck" is a huge mistake. Even if no one brings it to your attention, someone will know eventually, so tell your case representative right away. This person will, in all likelihood, initially accuse you of impropriety. They may say that you did not report changes in your circumstances, or say you gave them incomplete or even incorrect information. Keep copies of everything! If you can show them proof that you were not at fault, they may not make you pay back anything. There is an appeals process, so if you have trouble, ask your SSA rep for a waiver called an "SSA-632." They may try to dissuade you or even flat out deny you the right to a waiver, but do not take no for an answer. It is your right to ask for this form! When you get it, document why you feel this mistake was not your fault and show how having to pay back an overpayment may cause you or your family undue hardship. This simply means the SSA will need documentation (bills and other related documents) to show how you use benefits to meet all of your monthly expenses. If you are not sure about what caused the overpayment, ask to see detailed case file information and have the representative explain everything fully. Do not have them explain over the phone. If they tell you this is the best way to go, know that it is only the "best" course for them – not for you. Understand that if you take over payments and do not say anything, the SSA will have just cause to stop your (or your child's) benefits and close the case. Their Web site states that they will give you 30 days to pay the money back. Do not count on it! It may take more than that to receive a notice in the mail. If you are not aware that you have received continual overpayment, the SSA has no personal stake in your case, and they will not care to hear "I did not receive notice in the mail." Keep track of all the paper work as well as documentation you receive. Know that it is not the SSA representative's job to protect you or others who receive SSI benefits. Truthfully, they have no personal stake in your case, and they will not care if your case is closed. It is unfortunate to consider that a mentally disabled person, for example, needs to be required to have the capacity to engage in verbal discourse with an SSA representative. Additionally, someone who is severely physically disabled may not be able to pick up a phone. If either disabled person, given the overpayment circumstance, has someone else caring for them, it is the assumption that the caregiver is on top of things or even competent. It is also the assumption that the caregiver will not take advantage of the disabled person. Often times, money becomes the central focus for those charged in caring for disabled individuals. They may even take advantage until the well runs dry.

Overpayment Case Example

According to a Social Security advocacy group from Montana, a man named "Rick" received Social Security Disability Insurance benefits for some time. He was also employed as a security guard. Because of a loop-hole in the Social Security system, the man received an overpayment notice from SSA stating that he owed $8,000. Rick was so upset by what had transpired that he contacted this advocacy group to get help. At the prompting of this group, he filed a request for reconsideration. It was found that SSA had mistakenly sent Rick a letter. They had not applied his medical Impairment Related Work Expense (IRWE). Because of this, it was determined that Rick had not been overpaid.

SECTION I: A BRIEF LOOK AT REVIEWS AND APPEALS

What If I Get Better?

After a person has been approved for benefits they will have to go through periodic reviews. Benefits will continue while the review process is conducted. There are two types: a medically continuing disability review and a work continuing disability review. The frequency of any continuing disability review (CDR) has to do with how bad your disability is and how long it might last. The SSA also considers how likely you are to recover. For disabilities that are considered by the SSA to be less severe, reviews can take place about every six to 18 months or so. A person's age may have something to do with this, too. If the disability is considered more severe, a review happens about every seven years. Upon initial acceptance into any benefits program, a person is supposed to receive an award letter. This letter has information in it as to when the first review will take place. Again, it is important that you keep any documentation you receive.

During the medically continuing disability review process, a medical consultant, typically a doctor, and a disability examiner reexamine the case file. They will both want to know what medical treatment you have received up to that point, so keep any hospital, clinic, or other type documentation you may have been given. This is to see if the disability still limits you somehow and if the disability has generated new problems for you. They may ask, "Do you have new symptoms?" If you are still limited or have new symptoms brought about by the initial disability, the two examiners will want to know how you are affected and in what way. Keeping this factor in mind between reviews may help you gather the appropriate information to help you when a review comes around. Sometimes, disability benefits are paid to people who can still work. The disability examiner may want to know what work, if any, you have been able to get. As of January 2002, if a person has been receiving benefits for two or more years, the SSA will not necessarily discontinue benefits if a person goes back to work. This determination is made during the work continuing disability review. During this type of review, the SSA looks to see if you are still within the income limits to receive benefits. If you make too much money, you might lose the benefits altogether.

Ticket to Work Program

The Ticket to Work Program is a vocational rehabilitation program that was initiated in 1999. It was designed to help those who receive disability benefits become more financially self-sufficient. Under this program, a disability beneficiary can volunteer to take part in services, provided by the SSA, that they think will better their employment opportunities. Anyone who is between 18 and 64 years old may be eligible. An effort was made by the SSA to amend the program September 2005:

We are proposing to revise our regulations for the Ticket to Work and Self-Sufficiency Program (Ticket to Work program), authorized by the Ticket to Work and Work Incentives Improvement Act of 1999. The Ticket to Work program provides beneficiaries with disabilities expanded options for access to employment services, vocational rehabilitation services, and other support services. We are proposing to make revisions to the current rules to improve the overall effectiveness of the program in assisting beneficiaries to maximize their economic self-sufficiency through work opportunities. These revisions are based on our vision of the future direction of the Ticket to Work program, our experience using the current rules, and recommendations made by a number of commenters on the program (Federal Register: September 30, 2005 (Volume 70, Number 189).

Denied

According to some statistics, a majority of Social Security disability cases are initially denied. Many of these cases are reversed upon appeal, however. The process can be arduous, and some appeals have been known to last for several months or even years. Try not to panic, and definitely do not give up. There are some precautions that you can take to prevent your case from being denied.

A common reason that a disability examiner may deny a case is if a person's file is incomplete or inaccurate. For example, if, upon filing your initial application, you lived at address "A," and for some reason you move soon afterward to address "B," and you do not notify anyone, the SSA has no way to contact you. It is not their job to find you, and they will not come looking. Not reporting any changes in your case status is a guaranteed way to get denied. Another mistake people make is they do not do as they are told. If a disability examiner needs extra information about your medical history, give it to them. Do not say something like, *"I gave you everything already! Can't you do your job?"* Even if they find your complaint is justified, an examiner will not waste his or her time fighting. If on the phone, for example, do not be surprised if he or she hangs up on you. Many people threaten or argue with reps, but one moment of misdirected hostility could leave you in ruin. Some people say that when presented with a situation like this, ask for a supervisor. Do not wait until a situation becomes heated before having valuable information you might need later. It is better to get a supervisor's name and number before things turn bad. At some point, you will have to have contact with a "person" before they can deny your application. When you initially apply, be as polite as possible and say that you would like relevant information (names, numbers, and e-mail addresses) for informational purposes. For example: *"Oh, I just need it in case I have a question later and you are not available."* Write everything down and save it for later. In some circumstances, a rep will casually try to redirect you to the SSA Web site. He or she may even say his or her computer is "down." This is when "person-to-person" contact works best. Linger for as long as you can to get the information you need. They will do anything not to have to deal with you for too long!

Fraud is a third major factor that can result in a case being denied. People who knowingly get benefits by outright deception should be prepared for serious consequences. If you have tried to receive benefits fraudulently for someone else, the SSA may have the right to sanction that person permanently. Social Security also reports fraud to the police.

Appeals Process

If benefits are terminated, denied, or if a person does not agree with an SSA decision, the person may appeal. This simply means a person formally requests that the SSA reconsider their decision. There are four steps to this process. The first is called "request for reconsideration." According to the SSA, this step is done by someone who did not take part in an initial decision. For example, if a person's case was denied, an SSA third party re-reviews information from the case. In most circumstances, the SSA will not require that an applicant be present during the reconsideration. The second step in the appeals process is called a "hearing." The SSA will allow an administrative judge to hear the details about a case. According to the *Social Security Handbook*, during this portion of the process, a person has the right to be heard directly, and he or she can bring his or her own witnesses to be heard. This includes any medical professionals, too. If you have a doctor ready to be a witness for you, make a great effort to bring him or her. Often times, judges defer to doctors' medical experience, especially if they are reputable or well-known. If for some reason you cannot attend the hearing, you have to let the SSA office know why. In some situations, they will allow you to attend the hearing via phone or video conferencing. It may be a good idea to have representation, if you are able. The "Appeals Council" is the third step in the series of the appeals process. The Appeals Council is a group that reviews certain cases. This is done after the hearing process has already been completed, but the council reserves the right to deny a case if they feel it has already been decided correctly. For example, let us say that during the hearing process a decision is made. Procedure dictates that a person then gets a decision letter in the mail. This information is also forwarded to the Appeals Council when a person feels the hearing process decision is not correct. Simply, the council will not reconsider a case they feel has already been decided correctly. If the Appeals Council denies a case or refuses to reconsider it at all, you may have the option to file a lawsuit in federal district court. Typically, throughout the appeals process, the SSA will send you letters during each step to let you know what your options are at that point. Take care to collect everything you receive. In some circumstances, a person may ask to keep receiving benefits (if they have not already been taken away, that is) for the duration of the appeals process. After that the initial notice (the first one you get that says your benefits are going to stop), you have ten days to file your appeal. If you make this window, the SSA will probably grant your request to keep receiving benefits until a final determination is made.

Did You Know?

The United States Supreme Court will only hear court cases that have to do with a wide range of legal issues regarding constitutionality. Unlike lower courts, the Supreme Court's job is not to decide cases on an individual basis, but to decide if certain cases affect a wide range of other cases. In many circumstances the Supreme Court is even reluctant (called "judicial self restraint") to hear cases because of the scope of their power. Rulings from this court could affect the outcomes of many other cases across the country for years to come. Article III of the Constitution called "Cases and Controversies" helps determine whether it is appropriate for the Supreme Court hear a case at all. A major deciding factor has to do with whether or not cases have been first heard by a lower court. The main thing here is to try and establish if a case has been brought through the legal system already. Interestingly, there is little the Supreme Court can do to enforce any decision they make.

SUMMARY

Chapter 3 covers:

Disability Benefits: This section defines disability as "inability to engage in any substantial gainful activity by reason of any medically determinable physical or mental impairment which can be expected to result in death or has lasted or can be expected to last for a continuous period of not less than 12 months." It talks about the two main programs.

Social Security Disability Insurance (SSDI): SSDI is the program that gives benefits to adults who are impaired because of a medical condition. This condition should be anticipated to last for a lengthy period, and the income requirement range is more than for SSI.

Supplemental Security Income (SSI): SSI is a similar program to SSDI; however it maintains a less stringent income and resource requirement for those who qualify.

Presumptive Disability: A type of benefit an applicant may receive while an initial disability application is in the works.

Conditional Benefits: If you are not eligible for presumptive or other benefits under SSI, you may qualify to get a loan from the SSA.

Reviews and Appeals: This section gives a brief overview about how reviews and appeals work. If benefits are terminated, denied, or if a person does not agree with an SSA decision, they may appeal. This simply means a person formally requests that the SSA reconsider their decision. There are four steps to this process.

Ticket to Work Program: The Ticket to Work Program is a vocational rehabilitation program that was initiated in 1999. It was designed to help those who receive disability benefits become more financially self-sufficient.

Denied: According to some statistics, a majority of Social Security disability cases are initially denied. Many of these cases are reversed upon appeal. However, the process can be arduous, and some appeals have been known to last for several months or even years.

Overpayments: SSA can sometimes overestimate the amount of income you will receive over a given period. They call this difference between what is due and what is received "overpayment." Know that you will be responsible for paying back the dollar amount owed. However, there are circumstances when SSA incorrectly calculates dollar sums.

4

OTHER PROGRAMS & BENEFITS

SECTION I: DEPENDENT BENEFITS

What Is a "Dependent?"

The word "dependent" refers to a family member who counts on a certain amount of support (not always only financial) from someone else. This refers to people who live under the same roof, but not always. A dependent is considered someone who is not self-reliant, and whose well-being is contingent on the status of his or her provider. Simply, if you take care of, or are responsible for, someone else, they are your dependent. If you have kids or other relatives you provide for, for example, they can be considered to be your "dependents." They may also be termed as your "qualifying child" or "qualifying relatives" under the law as defined by the Internal Revenue Service (IRS).

What Are Dependent Benefits?

Dependent Benefits can only be given to those who financially depend on a beneficiary. For example, if a parent receives Social Security benefits of some type, their children would probably qualify. Both biological children and stepchildren qualify under this condition. Primarily, if either type of those children are dependents of a beneficiary under either the Retirement or Disability programs, they qualify if they are unmarried, under 18 years old, or if they are a student between the ages of 18 and 19 (22 years old, if disabled). According to the SSA, about three months before your qualifying child turns 18, you will receive notification that benefits will stop. If you child is still in high school, but over 18 years old, there are some conditions when benefits are kept in place until the child graduates from high school. The SSA will require some verification of this, however. Some kind of confirmation from a reliable school official will suffice as proper confirmation.

How Much Can They Get?

According to the Social Security Handbook a child may receive "up to one half of a parent's full retirement or disability benefit or 75 percent of dead parent's basic Social Security benefit." This amount can be around 160 percent of whatever the full benefit has been determined. Additional information in this handbook also states that if benefits payable exceed this percentage amount, the amount a family may receive in dependent benefits may temporarily be reduced until the payable amount no longer exceeds the maximum payable amount. If applying for SSDI, this amount is again determined by an earnings record, so benefits vary from person to person.

How Do I Protect Them?

According to the SSA, a child that is protected under the dependent benefits program must be the biological, adopted, or stepchild of the insured (or beneficiary of an SSA program). In some circumstances, a child that has not been legally established by the insured may still be able to get dependent benefits. This has to have been established sometime prior to when you apply. For example, a person cannot try to get dependent benefits for someone, and then turn around and try to establish that child is a dependent at the same time – not if a person wants to receive dependent benefits for someone else, that is. There must be reasonable evidence the child is, according to the SSA, the child of the insured. If a child is born illegitimately, for example, they can still qualify for dependent benefits. One such example would be if this child at one point lived with the person who is insured under the SSA. There are also benefits in the event either the insured person or an established dependent is deceased.

SECTION II: SURVIVOR BENEFITS

A common reason why people get Survivor Benefits

is to protect loved ones financially in the event of an unexpected death. No one wants to think about what will happen when someone we love dies. The loss can be devastating. This loss can be doubly harsh if a person and their family are left unprepared.

What Is It?

The term "survivor" means "a person who outlives another and obtains an interest in the property of a deceased person." Under this definition, this typically refers to living relatives of a family member, a "wage-earner," according to the SSA, such as a spouse or dependent children. In 1939, new amendments to the Social Security Act expanded coverage to include these types of benefits. The way the program works is that typically the worker, prior to his or her death, earns a certain amount of work credits for the duration he or she was employed. The amount of money the family may receive is contingent on how many years the deceased worker was in the workforce. This is determined by averaging the worker's earnings over his or her lifetime. The standard amount of time a worker needs to have been employed, according to the SSA, is about ten years. According to SSA statistics, 98 percent of families who apply for death benefits are approved provided they meet certain criteria.

Who Qualifies?

If you are a spouse 65 years old or older, you may receive

full benefits under this program. In some circumstances a surviving spouse may even receive full benefits as early as 50 years old. For divorced spouses, the SSA requires that you need to have been married to the deceased worker for at least ten years before you may become eligible. For children, they may receive death benefits if they are 16 years old or younger. Those children who also qualify should be unmarried and less than 18 years old. Children who were disabled before they were 22 years old may receive benefits at any age. Surviving dependent parents may also qualify.

How Do I Get It?

Anyone seeking benefits can apply by the regular avenues – by telephone, on the Internet, or by going to their local SSA offices. According to the SSA, people who want to apply for survivor benefits should do so as early as possible. The documentation families need when applying include a death certificate, marriage certificate, Social Security numbers for all family members, the deceased worker's tax return, and bank account information, if applicable. If you were receiving Social Security benefits prior to your family member dying, the SSA will change your status. This just means you will then fall under the Survivor Benefits program instead. Some programs under this portion of Social Security include: monthly widow or widower insurance benefits, monthly surviving child insurance benefits, monthly mother or father insurance benefits, monthly parent insurance benefits, and lump sum death payment.

What Is a Lump Sum Death Payment?

This type of payment is a single payment, rather than a division of payments, made to a surviving spouse upon the death of an insured worker. According to the SSA, a surviving spouse may be eligible to receive a one-time lump sum death payment of $255. The worker must have had a certain amount of earned credit to qualify survivors for this type of payment. The main condition to receive this benefit requires that the survivor had to have lived with the deceased at some point – at the time the person died. If the deceased worker was not married at the time of his or her death, this payment may go to a dependent child of the deceased. The added requirement for children is they need to have been on the deceased worker's earning record within the month of his or her death.

Special Coverage Provisions

According to the SSA, some occupations are not covered under general Social Security programs and have even been excluded, by law, from being able to receive certain benefits all together. They can, however, qualify for some protection under certain or special conditions. Agricultural and domestic labor are two such occupations that fall under this category. According to the Social Security Handbook, agricultural labor is defined as "work performed as the operation, management, conservation, improvement, or maintenance of a farm and its tools or equipment." For farmers, only cash pay is counted toward Social Security taxes provided "the cash was paid to you by your employer whose expenditures for agricultural labor are $2,500 or the cash pay paid to you in a calendar year for agricultural labor by one employer amounts to $150 or more (the cash-pay test) if your employer spends less than $2,500 in the year for agricultural labor." Domestic labor is defined as "work performed as an essential part of household duties," and this includes caretakers, babysitters, cooks, and house cleaners. For babysitters, there are two distinctions under the law that may determine whether or not they fall into an employee/employer relationship, which is something that I will detail later in Chapter 5. It basically says the law has to establish that an employer/employee relationship exists before they can get taxes from you. The government taxes an independent contractor differently than they would an "employee" or "employer," for example. The first distinction has to do with where the babysitter cares for a child. For example, if a babysitter cares for a child in the "child home," the babysitter is subject to taxes under an employee/employer relationship (more about this definition in Chapter 5). If the babysitter cares for a child in his or her own home, then the sitter is not found to fall under the employer/employee category. If this is the case, the sitter pays taxes in another fashion. This may be one of the reasons why a person who has a domestic job may be excluded from some Social Security benefits, but again, they may qualify under Special Provisions.

Special Veterans Benefits

According to the Social Security Handbook, "Special Veterans Benefits" are the type of benefits issued to World War II veterans who typically live outside the United States. To be eligible to receive this type of benefits, the SSA requires that a person be 65 years old or older on December 14, 1999. This was the day the law was enacted. A person must file an application, be a World War II veteran, be eligible for SSI, and not have another source of benefit income that "exceeds 75 percent" of the federal limit for SSI. If you return to the United States to live, your benefits will stop.

SUMMARY

Chapter 4 covers:

Dependent benefits: This section gives the SSA definition of what a dependent is and explains who may be considered a "qualifying" child or other relative under the law. Dependent Benefits can only be given to those who financially depend on a beneficiary.

Survivor benefits: This section talks about what survivor benefits are and who qualifies to receive help. The term "survivor" means "a person who outlives another and obtains an interest in the property of a deceased person." Under this definition, this refers to living relatives of a family member, a "wage-earner," according to the SSA, such as a spouse or dependent children.

Lump sum payments: Refers to a single or one-time benefit payout under the Survivor Benefits Social Security program. This type of payment is a single payment, rather than a division of payments, made to a surviving spouse upon the death of an insured worker. According to the SSA, a surviving spouse may be eligible to receive a one-time lump sum death payment of $255.

Special Coverage Provisions: According to the SSA, some occupations are not covered under general Social Security programs and have even been excluded, by law, from being able to receive benefits all together. They can, however, qualify for some protection under certain or special conditions. Agricultural and domestic labor are two such occupations that fall under this category.

Special Veterans benefits: Refers to Social Security programs for World War II veterans living outside the United States. To be eligible to receive this type of benefit, the SSA requires that a person be 65 years old or older on December 14, 1999.

"Expect nothing, live frugally on surprise."

Alice Walker

EMPLOYER/EMPLOYEE RESPONSIBILITIES

WHAT IS AN EMPLOYER/EMPLOYEE RELATIONSHIP?

What most people do not know is there has not always been a clear distinction as to what constitutes and an "employer" or "employee." Because of previous court cases (1947 and on) involving the U.S Treasury Department, the Supreme Court and the Department of Health and Human Services (formerly the Federal Security Agency), some technical definitions of these terms are now a matter of legal record. Interestingly, the original Social Security Act did not make a clear distinction between what an "employee" or "employer" was legally. It was not until the IRS later, around 1937, initially defined an employee as "an officer of a corporation" that these terms found meaning. But not everyone can be categorized in this manner, so what do these terms mean today?

According to former U.S law, an employee/employer relationship is defined as: *"if under the usual common-law rules the relationship between him and the person for whom he performs services is the legal relationship of employer and employee."* SSA policy makes this definition a little more concise as: "an employee if he is subject to the right of direction and control by the person for whom his services are performed as to the details and means by which the result is accomplished." According to the new *Social Security Handbook*, you are defined as an "employer" if you "have the final authority or right to control workers in performing their services, including hiring, firing, and supervising."

A person reading this book may wonder why anyone would waste so much time with what may seem like arbitrary nonsense. For the most part it has to do with money. The government cannot tax an employee or employer if he or she has not clearly established what he or she means ahead of time. Because these terms were reevaluated in 1978 by Congress, the IRS is not allowed to tax certain people under certain circumstances today.

Before I start talking about what an employer does or what an employee's responsibilities are regarding Social Security taxes, and benefits, let me back up a minute. As I said before, Social Security keeps a running tally of the money you pay into taxes for the duration of your work history – the 35 years in which you made the most money. This information is kept on your earnings record or statement. The amount of credits a person can earn on this statement can vary between men and women, which is something I will detail later in this section. Overall, people get this information upon request, but SSA sends periodic statements in the mail after you turn 25 years old. From the dollar amounts of those 35 years, SSA applies a standard formula to calculate the amount of benefits a person is eligible to receive from data listed on the record. Something that you should keep in mind is that there is a lost of "assuming" going on – on the part of SSA, that is. What I mean is that if you earned a certain amount of money for let us say, the year 2005, SSA will probably assume that you will make the same for the year 2006, 2007, and so on. It is important that your work earnings are correct. If, for some reason, you have not reported your income, there may be little that SSA can do to help you get the benefits you need when the time comes. There may be also little they could do to help family members if you were to die unexpectedly, given those circumstances. There is no way around it, everyone at some point will either retire or die. Here are some things you need to know to help yourself.

What Is a Worker to Do?

Know that both you and your employer are equally responsible for paying Social Security taxes. According to *The Complete Idiot's Guide to Social Security and Medicare*, about 7.65 percent of your income is taken out of your paycheck toward that purpose. The government takes 6.2 percent toward Social Security and 1.45 percent of your income goes to Medicare. That also means your employer needs to pay 7.65 percent, as well. The employer has to match whatever you pay, but they get to write off this money as a business expense on their taxes. The rules are a little different if you are self-employed, according to the guide. What does that mean? Those people who own their own business are responsible for both ends, meaning they are considered both "employer" and "employee" and their share amounts to about 15.3 percent of income. Self-employed people get to also deduct the amount of money they pay, too. They can claim about half of that same amount as a business expense. So what is a worker to do?

WHAT EMPLOYEES SHOULD KNOW

If you have ever had a job before, you probably know what a W-4 form looks like. An employer is required to give every new employee this piece of paper when they are first hired. It is technically referred to as an "Employee Withholding Allowance Certificate." It is a way for the government to know something about your living and financial situation. They may refer to this as "exemption status." It is also a way for them to categorize you. If your circumstances change, you may consider re-filing every year whether you change jobs or not. It might help you in the end. Depending on what exemptions you claim, this will determine how you are categorized and will also determine what deductions you will eventually be able to see on your paychecks. As I stated earlier, this is what is commonly referred to as the "Federal Contributions Insurance Act" or "FICA." Medicare, which I will detail later, is also a secondary amount deducted.

A little trick to remember when filling out this form is to think about how much money you want right away. When people fill out this form, if they want to receive more money in the year, they claim the most of their allowable exemptions. If they want to receive a larger amount of money when they file taxes, meaning at the end of the year, they should claim the least allowable amount of exemptions. For example, if you are a single mom with two kids, you probably can claim four exemptions if you want your money right away. In contrast, if you are that single mom and want a larger sum of money at the end of the year, you should claim a smaller amount. Sometimes people even claim "0" exemptions depending on their circumstances. You will not "save" any money on taxes. If you get money at the end of the year, what essentially happens is that during the course of that year, you are letting the government borrow the use of your money. They have to pay you back, but without paying you interest. Again, how much you get is contingent on what you want to have happen.

W-4s can be a little confusing, especially if you are young. When I was a freshman in college, I got a job at a pizzeria and I remember my employer making me fill out this form. I did not know anything about what it was for, nor did I care. I just trusted my employer had my best interest at heart and after filling it out, I never gave the information a second thought. Often times, this is the case with many people. Unfortunately, when you get older, if you still remain ignorant, it may cost you in the end. So, what is an exemption status? How do the categories work?

The government primarily categorizes you by how much money you make. They have a set table of dollars and from that set table, they take a certain percent out for taxes. According to the SSA Web site, if you made up to $97,500 for 2007, SSA will take 6.2 percent. For 2008 that number can go up a bit to a whopping $102,000 and you will still be responsible for that 6.2 percent. The numbers will still remain the same for Medicare at 1.45 percent.

Who makes that much money? Most people I know are way under those respective amounts, but the numbers might still apply. From those numbers, SSA determines how many credits you may earn toward being able to receive future benefits. For 2007, according to the SSA Web site, every $1,000 earned equals "one" credit for a maximum of four credits a year. Remember, a person needs to have earned 40 credits for the duration of his or her work history to be able to receive certain types of benefits. For 2008, a person needs $1,050 to earn one credit. If you are already receiving Social Security benefits, know numbers may vary according to your age and birth date. The government says that once an employee completes this form and returns it to his or her employer, he or she has fulfilled the reporting obligation by law. The next step is up to your employer, but make sure they have done their bit correctly, too!

WHAT YOUR EMPLOYER SHOULD KNOW

If you have a business and employ others, I am sure you know the government is going to get its money from you. Typically, when an employer starts a business they get a Tax ID number from the government. An employer is also required to get all corresponding information from their employee (name, Social Security number, and so forth). They will need to enter this information on a W-2 form, otherwise known as a "Wage and Tax Statement," and submit this information appropriately. In some circumstances, the employer has to open a business bank account (sometimes under the Tax ID number) and make monthly deposits into that account. That money should consist of your matched dollar amounts – by the 15th of every month. Also, that money is sent directly to the IRS and then you report whatever you sent to them to the Social Security Administration. Employers additionally have to make quarterly reports. The forms are called "941" or for federal employers a "940." Both

W-4 FORM

Form W-4 (2008)

Purpose. Complete Form W-4 so that your employer can withhold the correct federal income tax from your pay. Consider completing a new Form W-4 each year and when your personal or financial situation changes.

Exemption from withholding. If you are exempt, complete **only** lines 1, 2, 3, and 7 and sign the form to validate it. Your exemption for 2008 expires February 16, 2009. See Pub. 505, Tax Withholding and Estimated Tax.

Note. You cannot claim exemption from withholding if (a) your income exceeds $900 and includes more than $300 of unearned income (for example, interest and dividends) and (b) another person can claim you as a dependent on their tax return.

Basic instructions. If you are not exempt, complete the **Personal Allowances Worksheet** below. The worksheets on page 2 adjust your withholding allowances based on itemized deductions, certain credits,

adjustments to income, or two-earner/multiple job situations. Complete all worksheets that apply. However, you may claim fewer (or zero) allowances.

Head of household. Generally, you may claim head of household filing status on your tax return only if you are unmarried and pay more than 50% of the costs of keeping up a home for yourself and your dependent(s) or other qualifying individuals. See Pub. 501, Exemptions, Standard Deduction, and Filing Information, for information.

Tax credits. You can take projected tax credits into account in figuring your allowable number of withholding allowances. Credits for child or dependent care expenses and the child tax credit may be claimed using the **Personal Allowances Worksheet** below. See Pub. 919, How Do I Adjust My Tax Withholding, for information on converting your other credits into withholding allowances.

Nonwage income. If you have a large amount of nonwage income, such as interest or dividends, consider making estimated tax

payments using Form 1040-ES, Estimated Tax for Individuals. Otherwise, you may owe additional tax. If you have pension or annuity income, see Pub. 919 to find out if you should adjust your withholding on Form W-4 or W-4P.

Two earners or multiple jobs. If you have a working spouse or more than one job, figure the total number of allowances you are entitled to claim on all jobs using worksheets from only one Form W-4. Your withholding usually will be most accurate when all allowances are claimed on the Form W-4 for the highest paying job and zero allowances are claimed on the others. See Pub. 919 for details.

Nonresident alien. If you are a nonresident alien, see the Instructions for Form 8233 before completing this Form W-4.

Check your withholding. After your Form W-4 takes effect, use Pub. 919 to see how the dollar amount you are having withheld compares to your projected total tax for 2008. See Pub. 919, especially if your earnings exceed $130,000 (Single) or $180,000 (Married).

Personal Allowances Worksheet (Keep for your records.)

A Enter "1" for **yourself** if no one else can claim you as a dependent . . . . **A** _____

B Enter "1" if:
- You are single and have only one job; or
- You are married, have only one job, and your spouse does not work; or
- Your wages from a second job or your spouse's wages (or the total of both) are $1,500 or less. } . . **B** _____

C Enter "1" for your **spouse**. But, you may choose to enter "-0-" if you are married and have either a working spouse or more than one job. (Entering "-0-" may help you avoid having too little tax withheld.) . . . . . . **C** _____

D Enter number of **dependents** (other than your spouse or yourself) you will claim on your tax return . . . . **D** _____

E Enter "1" if you will file as **head of household** on your tax return (see conditions under **Head of household** above) . **E** _____

F Enter "1" if you have at least $1,500 of **child or dependent care expenses** for which you plan to claim a credit . **F** _____
(**Note.** Do **not** include child support payments. See Pub. 503, Child and Dependent Care Expenses, for details.)

G **Child Tax Credit** (including additional child tax credit). See Pub. 972, Child Tax Credit, for more information.
- If your total income will be less than $58,000 ($86,000 if married), enter "2" for each eligible child.
- If your total income will be between $58,000 and $84,000 ($86,000 and $119,000 if married), enter "1" for each eligible child plus "1" **additional** if you have 4 or more eligible children. . . . . **G** _____

H Add lines A through G and enter total here. (**Note.** This may be different from the number of exemptions you claim on your tax return.) ▶ **H** _____

| For accuracy, complete all worksheets that apply. | • If you plan to **itemize or claim adjustments to income** and want to reduce your withholding, see the **Deductions and Adjustments Worksheet** on page 2.
• If you have more than one job or are **married and you and your spouse both work** and the combined earnings from all jobs exceed $40,000 ($25,000 if married), see the **Two-Earners/Multiple Jobs Worksheet** on page 2 to avoid having too little tax withheld.
• If **neither** of the above situations applies, **stop here** and enter the number from line H on line 5 of Form W-4 below. |

- - - - - - - - - - **Cut here and give Form W-4 to your employer. Keep the top part for your records.** - - - - - - - - - -

Form **W-4**
Department of the Treasury
Internal Revenue Service

Employee's Withholding Allowance Certificate

▶ **Whether you are entitled to claim a certain number of allowances or exemption from withholding is subject to review by the IRS. Your employer may be required to send a copy of this form to the IRS.**

OMB No. 1545-0074

2008

1 Type or print your first name and middle initial. | Last name | **2** Your social security number

Home address (number and street or rural route)

3 ☐ Single ☐ Married ☐ Married, but withhold at higher Single rate.
Note. If married, but legally separated, or spouse is a nonresident alien, check the "Single" box.

City or town, state, and ZIP code

4 If your last name differs from that shown on your social security card, check here. You must call 1-800-772-1213 for a replacement card. ▶ ☐

5 Total number of allowances you are claiming (from line **H** above **or** from the applicable worksheet on page 2) | **5** _____

6 Additional amount, if any, you want withheld from each paycheck . . . . | **6** $ _____

7 I claim exemption from withholding for 2008, and I certify that I meet **both** of the following conditions for exemption.
- Last year I had a right to a refund of **all** federal income tax withheld because I had **no** tax liability **and**
- This year I expect a refund of **all** federal income tax withheld because I expect to have **no** tax liability.
If you meet both conditions, write "Exempt" here . . . . ▶ | **7** _____

Under penalties of perjury, I declare that I have examined this certificate and to the best of my knowledge and belief, it is true, correct, and complete.
Employee's signature
(Form is not valid unless you sign it.) ▶   **Date** ▶

8 Employer's name and address (Employer: Complete lines 8 and 10 only if sending to the IRS.) | **9** Office code (optional) | **10** Employer identification number (EIN)

For Privacy Act and Paperwork Reduction Act Notice, see page 2. | Cat. No. 10220Q | Form **W-4** (2008)

To see the rest of this form, visit **http://www.irs.gov/pub/irs-pdf/fw4.pdf.**

the IRS and SSA have a way to check reported numbers, too. The "Employer Reconciliation Process" is a way for both agencies to keep track of wage dollars. If for some reason the dollars do not match – let us say the amount of money reported to SSA is different than the amount reported to the IRS – the employer will be responsible. According to SSA, if there is a large difference between the two numbers, a worker's earnings may not be reported correctly and the employee will not receive due earnings credit. This means if the employee at some point needs Social Security benefits, he or she may not receive his or her fair due. If there are huge discrepancies, SSA will attempt to find out what the problem is without contacting you, but if they cannot figure out what is going on, they will start sending notices immediately to remedy the issue. Those letters are commonly referred to as "no match" letters. They fall into two categories. The first is typically sent by SSA to an employer and it is called an "Employer Correction Request and Educational Response" (EDCOR). The second, sent by SSA to employees, is called a "Decentralized Correspondence" (DECOR) letter. If for some reason, an employee cannot be reached, SSA will send this correspondence to the worker's employer. Know that if SSA contacts you and you do not respond, they will submit information to the IRS who will invariably then come after you. The way they do this is by imposing penalties (charging you money on top of the amount you already have to pay). It is in your best interest to keep track of everything correctly. Whatever dollar amount you pay in those taxes can be a business expense, so report the numbers exactly. If you do not, you could suffer a big loss.

SOCIAL SECURITY ACT OF 1935: TITLE IX - TAX ON EMPLOYERS OF EIGHT OR MORE

IMPOSITION OF TAX

SECTION 901. On and after January 1, 1936, every employer (as defined in section 907) shall pay for each calendar year an excise tax, with respect to having individuals in his employ, equal to the following percentages of the total wages (as defined in section 907) payable by him (regardless of the time of payment) with respect to employment (as defined in section 907) during such calendar year:

(1) With respect to employment during the calendar year 1936 the rate shall be 1 per centum;

(2) With respect to employment during the calendar year 1937 the rate shall be 2 per centum;

(3) With respect to employment after December 31, 1937, the rate shall be 3 per centum.

CREDIT AGAINST TAX

SEC. 902. The taxpayer may credit against the tax imposed by section 901 the amount of contributions, with respect to employment during the taxable year, paid by him (before the date of filing of his return for the taxable year) into an unemployment fund under a State law. The total credit allowed to a taxpayer under this section for all contributions paid into unemployment funds with respect to employment during such taxable year shall not exceed 90 per centum of the tax against which it is credited, and credit shall be allowed only for contributions made under the laws of States certified for the taxable year as provided in section 903.

SOCIAL SECURITY ACT OF 1935: TITLE IX - TAX ON EMPLOYERS OF EIGHT OR MORE

CERTIFICATION OF STATE LAWS

SEC. 903. (a) The Social Security Board shall approve any State law submitted to it, within thirty days of such submission, which it finds provides that-

(1) All compensation is to be paid through public employment offices in the State or such other agencies as the Board may approve;

(2) No compensation shall be payable with respect to any day of unemployment occurring within two years after the first day of the first period with respect to which contributions are required;

(3) All money received in the unemployment fund shall immediately upon such receipt be paid over to the Secretary of the Treasury to the credit of the Unemployment Trust Fund established by section 904;

(4) All money withdrawn from the Unemployment Trust Fund by the State agency shall be used solely in the payment of compensation, exclusive of expenses of administration;

(5) Compensation shall not be denied in such State to any otherwise eligible individual for refusing to accept new work under any of the following conditions:

(A) If the position offered is vacant due directly to a strike, lockout, or other labor dispute;

(B) if the wages, hours, or other conditions of the work offered are substantially less favorable to the individual than those prevailing for similar work in the locality;

SOCIAL SECURITY ACT OF 1935: TITLE IX - TAX ON EMPLOYERS OF EIGHT OR MORE

(C) if as a condition of being employed the individual would be required to join a company union or to resign from or refrain from joining any bona-fide labor organization;

(6) All the rights, privileges, or immunities conferred by such law or by acts done pursuant thereto shall exist subject to the power of the legislature to amend or repeal such law at any time. The Board shall, upon approving such law, notify the Governor of the State of its approval.

(b) On December 31 in each taxable year the Board shall certify to the Secretary of the Treasury each State whose law it has previously approved, except that it shall not certify any State which, after reasonable notice and opportunity for hearing to the State agency, the Board finds has changed its law so that it no longer contains the provisions specified in subsection (a) or has with respect to such taxable year failed to comply substantially with any such provision.

(c) If, at any time during the taxable year, the Board has reason to believe that a State whose law it has previously approved, may not be certified under subsection (b), it shall promptly so notify the Governor of such State.

UNEMPLOYMENT TRUST FUND

SEC. 904. (a) There is hereby established in the Treasury of the United States a trust fund to be known as the Unemployment Trust Fund , hereinafter in this title called the Fund . The Secretary of the Treasury is authorized and directed to receive and hold in the Fund all moneys deposited therein by a State agency from a State unemployment fund. Such deposit may be made directly with the Secretary of the

SOCIAL SECURITY ACT OF 1935: TITLE IX - TAX ON EMPLOYERS OF EIGHT OR MORE

Treasury or with any Federal reserve bank or member bank of the Federal Reserve System designated by him for such purpose.

(b) It shall be the duty of the Secretary of the Treasury to invest such portion of the Fund as is not, in his judgment, required to meet current withdrawals. Such investment may be made only in interest-bearing obligations of the United States or in obligations guaranteed as to both principal and interest by the United States. For such purpose such obligations may be acquired

(1) on original issue at par, or

(2) by purchase of outstanding obligations at the market price. The purposes for which obligations of the United States may be is- sued under the Second Liberty Bond Act, as amended, are hereby extended to authorize the issuance at par of special obligations exclusively to the Fund. Such special obligations shall bear interest at a rate equal to the average rate of interest, computed as of the end of the calendar month next preceding the date of such issue, borne by all interest-bearing obligations of the United States then forming part of the public debt; except that where such average rate is not a multiple of one eighth of 1 per centum, the rate of interest of such special obligations shall be the multiple of one-eighth of 1 per centum next lower than such average rate. Obligations other than such special obligations may be acquired for the Fund only on such terms as to provide an investment yield not less than the yield which would be required in the case of special obligations if issued to the Fund upon the date of such acquisition.

SOCIAL SECURITY ACT OF 1935: TITLE IX - TAX ON EMPLOYERS OF EIGHT OR MORE

(c) Any obligations acquired by the Fund (except special obligations issued exclusively to the Fund) may be sold at the market price, and such special obligations may be redeemed at par plus accrued interest.

(d) The interest on, and the proceeds from the sale or redemption of, any obligations held in the Fund shall be credited to and form a part of the Fund.

(e) The Fund shall be invested as a single fund, but the Secretary of the Treasury shall maintain a separate book account for each State agency and shall credit quarterly on March 31, June 30, September 30, and December 31, of each year, to each account, on the basis of the average daily balance of such account, a proportionate part of the earnings of the Fund for the quarter ending on such date.

(f) The Secretary of the Treasury is authorized and directed to pay out of the Fund to any State agency such amount as it may duly requisition, not exceeding the amount standing to the account of such State agency at the time of such payment.

ADMINISTRATION, REFUNDS, AND PENALTIES

SEC. 905.

(a) The tax imposed by this title shall be collected by the Bureau of Internal Revenue under the direction of the Secretary of the Treasury and shall be paid into the Treasury of the United States as internal-revenue collections. If the tax is not paid when due, there shall be added as part of the tax interest at the rate of one-half of 1 per centum per month from the date the tax became due until paid.

SOCIAL SECURITY ACT OF 1935: TITLE IX - TAX ON EMPLOYERS OF EIGHT OR MORE

(b) Not later than January 31, next following the close of the taxable year, each employer shall make a return of the tax under this title for such taxable year. Each such return shall be made under oath, shall be filed with the collector of internal revenue for the district in which is located the principal place of business of the employer, or, if he has no principal place of business in the United States, then with the collector at Baltimore, Maryland, and shall contain such information and be made in such manner as the Commissioner of Internal Revenue, with the approval of the Secretary of the Treasury, may by regulations prescribe. All provisions of law (including penalties) applicable in respect of the taxes imposed by section 600 of the Revenue Act of 1926, shall, insofar as not inconsistent with this title, be applicable in respect of the tax imposed by this title. The Commissioner may extend the time for filing the return of the tax imposed by this title, under such rules and regulations as he may prescribe with the approval of the Secretary of the Treasury, but no such extension shall be for more than sixty days.

(c) Returns filed under this title shall be open to inspection in the same manner, to the same extent, and subject to the same provisions of law, including penalties, as returns made under Title II of the Revenue Act of 1926.

d) The taxpayer may elect to pay the tax in four equal installments instead of in a single payment, in which case the first installment shall be paid not later than the last day prescribed for the filing of returns, the second installment shall be paid on or before the last day of (the third month, the third installment on or before the last day of the sixth month, and the fourth installment on or before the

SOCIAL SECURITY ACT OF 1935: TITLE IX - TAX ON EMPLOYERS OF EIGHT OR MORE

last day of the ninth month, after such last day. If the tax or any installment thereof is not paid on or before the last day of the period fixed for its payment, the whole amount of the tax unpaid shall be paid upon notice and demand from the collector.

(e) At the request of the taxpayer the time for payment of the tax or any installment thereof may be extended under regulations prescribed by the Commissioner with the approval of the Secretary of the Treasury, for a period not to exceed six months from the last day of the period prescribed for the payment of the tax or any installment thereof. The amount of the tax in respect of which any extension is granted shall be paid (with interest at the rate of one-half of 1 per centum per month) on or before the date of the expiration of the period of the extension.

(f) In the payment of any tax under this title a fractional part of a cent shall be disregarded unless it amounts to one-half cent or more, in which case it shall be increased to 1 cent.

INTERSTATE COMMERCE

SEC. 906. No person required under a State law to make payments to an unemployment fund shall be relieved from compliance therewith on the ground that he is engaged in interstate commerce, or that the State law does not distinguish between employees engaged in interstate commerce and those engaged in intrastate commerce.

DEFINITIONS

SEC. 907. When used in this title --

(a) The term employer does not include any person unless on each of some twenty days during the taxable year, each day being a

SOCIAL SECURITY ACT OF 1935: TITLE IX - TAX ON EMPLOYERS OF EIGHT OR MORE

different calendar week, the total number of individuals who were in his employ for some portion of the day (whether or not at the same moment of time) was eight or more.

(b) The term wages means all remuneration for employment, including the cash value of all remuneration paid in any medium other than cash.

(c) The term employment means any service, of whatever nature, performed within the United States by an employee for his employer, except-

(1) Agricultural labor;

(2) Domestic service in a private home;

(3) Service performed as an officer or member of a crew of a vessel on the navigable waters of the United States;

(4) Service performed by an individual in the employ of his son, daughter, or spouse, and service performed by a child under the age of twenty-one in the employ of his father or mother;

(5) Service performed in the employ of the United States Government or of an instrumentality of the United States;

(6) Service performed in the employ of a State, a political subdivision thereof, or an instrumentality of one or more States or political subdivisions;

(7) Service performed in the employ of a corporation, community chest, fund, or foundation, organized and operated exclusively for religious, charitable, scientific, literary, or educational

SOCIAL SECURITY ACT OF 1935: TITLE IX - TAX ON EMPLOYERS OF EIGHT OR MORE

purposes, or for the prevention of cruelty to children or animals, no part of the net earnings of which inures to the benefit of any private shareholder or individual.

(d) The term State agency means any State officer, board, or other authority, designated under a State law to administer the unemployment fund in such State.

(e) The term unemployment fund means a special fund, established under a State law and administered by a State agency, for the payment of compensation.

(f) The term contributions means payments required by a State law to be made by an employer into an unemployment fund, to the extent that such payments are made by him without any part thereof being deducted or deductible from the wages of individuals in his employ.

(g) The term compensation means cash benefits payable to individuals with respect to their unemployment.

RULES AND REGULATIONS

SEC. 908. The Commissioner of Internal Revenue, with the approval of the Secretary of the Treasury, shall make and publish rules and regulations for the enforcement of this title, except sections 903, 904, and 910.

ALLOWANCE OF ADDITIONAL CREDIT

SEC. 909.

(a) In addition to the credit allowed under section 902, a taxpayer

SOCIAL SECURITY ACT OF 1935: TITLE IX - TAX ON EMPLOYERS OF EIGHT OR MORE

may, subject to the conditions imposed by section 910, credit against the tax imposed by section 901 for any taxable year after the taxable year 1937, an amount, with respect to each State law, equal to the amount, if any, by which the contributions, with respect to employment in such taxable year, actually paid by the taxpayer under such law before the date of filing his return for such taxable year, is exceeded by whichever of the following is the lesser- (1) The amount of contributions which he would have been required to pay under such law for such taxable year if he had been subject to the highest rate applicable from time to time throughout such year to any employer under such law; or (2) Two and seven-tenths per centum of the wages payable by him with respect to employment with respect to which contributions for such year were required under such law.

(b) If the amount of the contributions actually so paid by the taxpayer is less than the amount which he should have paid under the State law, the additional credit under subsection (a) shall be reduced proportionately.

(c) The total credits allowed to a taxpayer under this title shall not exceed 90 per centum of the tax against which such credits are taken.

CONDITIONS OF ADDITIONAL CREDIT ALLOWANCE

SEC. 910.

(a) A taxpayer shall be allowed the additional credit under section 909, with respect to his contribution rate under a State law being lower, for any taxable year, than that of another employer subject to such law, only if the Board finds that under such law--

SOCIAL SECURITY ACT OF 1935: TITLE IX - TAX ON EMPLOYERS OF EIGHT OR MORE

(1) Such lower rate, with respect to contributions to a pooled fund, is permitted on the basis of not less than three years of compensation experience;

(2) Such lower rate, with respect to contributions to a guaranteed employment account, is permitted only when his guaranty of employment was fulfilled in the preceding calendar year, and such guaranteed employment account amounts to not less than 7 « per centum of the total wages payable by him, in accordance with such guaranty, with respect to employment in such State in the preceding calendar year;

(3) Such lower rate, with respect to contributions to a separate reserve account, is permitted only when

(A) compensation has been payable from such account throughout the preceding calendar year, and

(B) such account amounts to not less than five times the largest amount of compensation paid from such account within any one of the three preceding calendar years, and

(C) such account amounts to not less than 7 per centum of the total wages payable by him (plus the total wages payable by any other employers who may be contributing to such account) with respect to employment in such State in the preceding calendar year.

(b) Such additional credit shall be reduced, if any contributions under such law are made by such taxpayer at a lower rate under

SOCIAL SECURITY ACT OF 1935: TITLE IX - TAX ON EMPLOYERS OF EIGHT OR MORE

conditions not fulfilling the requirements of subsection (a), by the amount bearing the same ratio to such additional credit as the amount of contributions made at such lower rate bears to the total of his contributions paid for such year under such law.

(c) As used in this section-

(1) The term reserve account means a separate account in an unemployment fund, with respect to an employer or group of employers, from which compensation is payable only with respect to the unemployment of individuals who were in the employ of such employer, or of one of the employers comprising the group. by employers with respect to whom reserve accounts are maintained by the State agency, it is payable only when such accounts are exhausted.

(2) The term pooled fund means an unemployment fund or any part thereof in which all contributions are mingled and undivided, and from which compensation is payable to all eligible individuals, except that to individuals last employed.

(3) The term guaranteed employment account means a separate account, in an unemployment fund, of contributions paid by an employer (or group of employers) who:

(A) guarantees in advance thirty hours of wages for each of forty calendar weeks (or more, with one weekly hour deducted for each added week guaranteed) in twelve months, to all the individuals in his employ in one or more distinct establishments, except that any such individuals

SOCIAL SECURITY ACT OF 1935: TITLE IX - TAX ON EMPLOYERS OF EIGHT OR MORE

guaranty may commence after a probationary period (included within twelve or less consecutive calendar weeks), and

(B) gives security or assurance, satisfactory to the State agency, for the fulfillment of such guaranties, from which account compensation shall be payable with respect to the unemployment of any such individual whose guaranty is not fulfilled or renewed and who is otherwise eligible for compensation under the State law.

(4) The term year of compensation experience , as applied to an employer, means any calendar year throughout which compensation was payable with respect to any individual in his employ who became unemployed and was eligible for compensation."

ARE YOU SELF EMPLOYED?

If you are self-employed, you will have a little more to contend with. As both employee and employer, the government will hold you responsible for "15.3 percent of your net earnings," according to the aforementioned *Idiot's Guide*. You may subtract one-half of that amount as the cost of doing business. That is one way to reduce the amount of taxes, called "a tax deduction," on the taxes you will have to eventually pay. The percentages work a little differently, as well. In 2007, for example, SSA says a self-employed person can earn up to $97,500 and pay 15.3 percent of the net earnings. If you make more than that, you only have to pay the Medicare portion of the Social Security tax, which amounts to about "2.9 percent on the rest of your earnings." Another way, according to SSA, that a self-employed person can get another tax deduction (again reducing your obligation further), is to "deduct half of your Social Security taxes on your 1040 tax form." They say to do this correctly, the amount must be from your gross earnings and "cannot be an itemized deduction and must not be listed on your schedule C." The Schedule C is simply a profit/loss sheet that a self-employed person has to send to the IRS. If you earn money from wages AND you are self-employed, SSA says you have to pay the taxes on the wages portion first. But it will not make much of a difference if your total annual income is not over $97,500. The SSA Web site gives a good example about how this could work. They say the rules might vary from year to year, but for 2006, if a person earns $20,000 in wages and $30,000 in self-employment income, a person is responsible for both taxes. SSA says that for the year 2007, if you make $70,000 in wages and $28,300 in net business income, you do not have to pay both taxes for incomes that exceed $97,500 annually. But remember – you are responsible for paying 15.3 percent of Social Security and Medicare taxes on the first $27,500 of your business earnings and 2.9 percent in Medicare on the $800 dollars remaining. This adds up to the $28,300 amount that I referred to earlier.

SCHEDULE C FORM

SCHEDULE C (Form 1040)

Department of the Treasury
Internal Revenue Service (99)

Profit or Loss From Business
(Sole Proprietorship)

► Partnerships, joint ventures, etc., must file Form 1065 or 1065-B.
► Attach to Form 1040, 1040NR, or 1041. ► See Instructions for Schedule C (Form 1040).

OMB No. 1545-0074

2007

Attachment Sequence No. 09

Name of proprietor

Social security number (SSN)

A Principal business or profession, including product or service (see page C-2 of the instructions)

B Enter code from pages C-8, 9 & 10 ►

C Business name. If no separate business name, leave blank.

D Employer ID number (EIN), if any

E Business address (including suite or room no.) ►
City, town or post office, state, and ZIP code

F Accounting method: (1) ☐ Cash (2) ☐ Accrual (3) ☐ Other (specify) ►

G Did you "materially participate" in the operation of this business during 2007? If "No," see page C-3 for limit on losses ☐ Yes ☐ No

H If you started or acquired this business during 2007, check here ► ☐

Part I Income

1	Gross receipts or sales. **Caution.** If this income was reported to you on Form W-2 and the "Statutory employee" box on that form was checked, see page C-3 and check here ► ☐	1
2	Returns and allowances	2
3	Subtract line 2 from line 1	3
4	Cost of goods sold (from line 42 on page 2)	4
5	**Gross profit.** Subtract line 4 from line 3	5
6	Other income, including federal and state gasoline or fuel tax credit or refund (see page C-3)	6
7	**Gross income.** Add lines 5 and 6 ►	7

Part II Expenses. Enter expenses for business use of your home **only** on line 30.

8	Advertising	8	18	Office expense	18
9	Car and truck expenses (see page C-4)	9	19	Pension and profit-sharing plans	19
10	Commissions and fees	10	20	Rent or lease (see page C-5):	
11	Contract labor (see page C-4)	11	a	Vehicles, machinery, and equipment	20a
12	Depletion	12	b	Other business property	20b
13	Depreciation and section 179 expense deduction (not included in Part III) (see page C-4)	13	21	Repairs and maintenance	21
			22	Supplies (not included in Part III)	22
			23	Taxes and licenses	23
			24	Travel, meals, and entertainment:	
14	Employee benefit programs (other than on line 19)	14	a	Travel	24a
15	Insurance (other than health)	15	b	Deductible meals and entertainment (see page C-6)	24b
16	Interest:		25	Utilities	25
a	Mortgage (paid to banks, etc.)	16a	26	Wages (less employment credits)	26
b	Other	16b	27	Other expenses (from line 48 on page 2)	27
17	Legal and professional services	17			

28	**Total expenses** before expenses for business use of home. Add lines 8 through 27 in columns ►	28
29	Tentative profit (loss). Subtract line 28 from line 7	29
30	Expenses for business use of your home. Attach **Form 8829**	30
31	**Net profit or (loss).** Subtract line 30 from line 29.	
	• If a profit, enter on both **Form 1040, line 12,** and **Schedule SE, line 2,** or on **Form 1040NR, line 13** (statutory employees, see page C-7). Estates and trusts, enter on Form 1041, line 3.	31
	• If a loss, you **must** go to line 32.	
32	If you have a loss, check the box that describes your investment in this activity (see page C-7).	
	• If you checked 32a, enter the loss on both **Form 1040, line 12,** and **Schedule SE, line 2,** or on **Form 1040NR, line 13** (statutory employees, see page C-7). Estates and trusts, enter on Form 1041, line 3.	32a ☐ All investment is at risk.
	• If you checked 32b, you **must** attach **Form 6198.** Your loss may be limited.	32b ☐ Some investment is not at risk.

For Paperwork Reduction Act Notice, see page C-8 of the instructions. Cat. No. 11334P Schedule C (Form 1040) 2007

THINGS TO KNOW ABOUT YOUR NET EARNINGS

According to SSA, a self-employed person may figure out his or her net business earnings by taking his or her gross earnings (everything they make) and subtracting his or her business deductions (costs of running your business, for example) and depreciation (something you have for the business that drops in value, for example). Know that in some circumstances, SSA will exclude certain items from those net earnings. Such items include things like dividends from shares of stock and interest on bonds, unless you receive them as a dealer in stocks and securities. Additionally, a self-employed person may deduct the interest from loans he or she receives or the value of rentals from real estate. The main restriction is that you cannot be in the "business" of lending money nor may you be a real-estate dealer.

If you are self-employed and you do not make a lot of money, SSA has an alternative method of filing Social Security tax. If a business owner's net earnings are less than $400 a year, he or she can still earn work credits toward Social Security. The government also says a person may also have a net income of $600 or more, provided his or her profit is less than $1,600 annually. You can earn up to $2,400, but may only use this alternative method five times during your entire work history. Farmers may use this method of reporting every year and the $400 a year restriction does not apply.

HIRING A FOREIGN EMPLOYEE

The first thing an employer should do when hiring a foreign employee is to have that person apply for a Social Security number right away, if they have not done so already. If you have hired this person, and they have not received a Social Security number by the time you file your wage report, SSA says to check the Applied For box on the W-2/W-3 application form. There are also alternatives to this for those employers who file electronically. Know that if you make a mistake, SSA has a way to correct most problems a prospective employer may experience.

BIAS OR NOT?

According to U.S. law, it is discriminatory to treat similar people in different ways. No one could reasonably argue, for example, that blue-eyed people are more efficient workers than brown-eyed people simply based on their eye color. They both could perform the tasks required, given that they are both equally "qualified" to do a job. Yes? Consider this:

A woman and a man both apply for a job. At the initial interview, a hiring manager asks the woman whether or not she is married and if she plans to have children. The manager also asks her plans regarding her daycare situation if and when she "chooses" to have those kids. The potential employer then asks if she presently has kids and if those kids are legitimate. The employer does not ask the man the same questions. Is this discriminatory?

Conversely, it is also unreasonable to presume that different people be treated equally. It would be unlawful to prevent a disabled person from having equal access to employment solely due to the fact that he or she is disabled. Disabled people have been legally identified as "different" and have subsequently been afforded due protection under the law. The Americans with Disabilities Act is an example of this.

A form of sex discrimination is when a woman is socially restricted to a certain status based solely on her gender. This restrictive status may even propel her into potentially undesirable situations, again, simply because she is a "woman." For example, how desirable would it be for a woman to remain unmarried when the only hope she can have for optimal long-term economic security is solely contingent on whether or not she has, at some point, been married. Is this biased?

The SSA Web site section entitled "What Every Woman Should Know," says men earn more money and ultimately generate more work credits toward their earnings statement. Remember, earnings statements pretty much dictate how much money someone can get when it comes time to apply for Social Security benefits. SSA says the reason that a woman does not statistically match men in this respect, is because women "tend" to leave their careers to have children or care for other people, as well. Additionally, a man can chose to remain unmarried and have children, while simultaneously remaining in the workforce. He is not penalized by SSA if he does this. He is still able to get the same amount of work credits that will ultimately provide for his future security. If a woman wishes to remain unmarried and have a child, for example, she is penalized, both socially and economically, by not having equal access to employment or to Social Security benefits. Equal access is only afforded when she remains childless and unmarried. A social stigma is also assigned to women who do this. Even if it is statistically viable, is it reasonable that both men and women are held to a similar economic work requirement, when in essence, they may be different? Is it biased or not?

SOCIAL SECURITY ACT OF 1935: TAXES WITH RESPECT TO EMPLOYMENT

INCOME TAX ON EMPLOYEES

SECTION 801. In addition to other taxes, there shall be levied, collected, and paid upon the income of every individual a tax equal to the following percentages of the wages (as defined in section 811) received by him after December 31, 1936, with respect to employment (as defined in section 811) after such date:

(1) With respect to employment during the calendar years 1937, 1938, and 1939, the rate shall be 1 per centum.

(2) With respect to employment during the calendar years 1940, 1941, and 1942, the rate shall 1 1/2 per centum.

(3) With respect to employment during the calendar years 1943, 1944, and 1945, the rate shall be 2 per centum.

(4) With respect to employment during the calendar years 1946, 1947, and 1948, the rate shall be 2 1/2 per centum.

(5) With respect to employment after December 31, 1948, the rate shall be 3 per centum.

SOCIAL SECURITY ACT OF 1935: TAXES WITH RESPECT TO EMPLOYMENT

DEDUCTION OF TAX FROM WAGES

SEC. 802.

(a) The tax imposed by section 801 shall be collected by the employer of the taxpayer by deducting the amount of the tax from the wages as and when paid. Every employer required so to deduct the tax is hereby made liable for the payment of such tax, and is hereby indemnified against the claims and demands of any person for the amount of any such payment made by such employer.

(b) If more or less than the correct amount of tax imposed by section 801 is paid with respect to any wage payment, then, under regulations made under this title, proper adjustments, with respect both to the tax and the amount to be deducted, shall be made, without interest, in connection with subsequent wage payments to the same individual by the same employer.

DEDUCTIBILITY FROM INCOME TAX

SEC. 803. For the purposes of the income tax imposed by Title I of the Revenue Act of 1934 or by any Act of Congress in substitution therefor, the tax imposed by section 801 shall not be allowed as a deduction to the taxpayer in computing his net income for the year in which such tax is deducted from his wages.

EXCISE TAX ON EMPLOYERS

SEC. 804. In addition to other taxes, every employer shall pay an excise tax, with respect to having individuals in his employ, equal to the following percentages of the wages (as defined in section 811) paid by him after December 31, 1936, with respect to employment (as defined in section 811) after such date:

SOCIAL SECURITY ACT OF 1935: TAXES WITH RESPECT TO EMPLOYMENT

(1) With respect to employment during the calendar years 1937, 1938, and 1939, the rate shall be 1 per centum.

(2) With respect to employment during the calendar years 1940, 1941, and 1942, the rate shall be 1 1/2 per centum.

(3) With respect to employment during the calendar years 1943, 1944, and 1945, the rate shall be 2 per centum.

(4) With respect to employment during the calendar years 1946, 1947, and 1948, the rate shall be 2 1/2 per centum.

(5) With respect to employment after December 31, 1948, the rate shall be 3 per centum.

ADJUSTMENT OF EMPLOYERS TAX

SEC. 805. If more or less than the correct amount of tax imposed by section 804 is paid with respect to any wage payment, then, under regulations made under this title, proper adjustments with respect the tax shall be made, without interest, in connection with subsequent wage payments to the same individual by the same employer.

REFUNDS AND DEFICIENCIES

SEC. 806. If more or less than the correct amount of tax imposed by section 801 or 804 is paid or deducted with respect to any wage payment and the overpayment or underpayment of tax cannot be adjusted under section 802 (b) or 805 the amount of the overpayment shall be refunded and the amount of the underpayment shall be collected in such manner and at such times (subject to the statutes of limitations properly applicable thereto) as may be prescribed by regulations made under this title.

SOCIAL SECURITY ACT OF 1935: TAXES WITH RESPECT TO EMPLOYMENT

COLLECTION AND PAYMENT OF TAXES

SEC. 807.

(a) The taxes imposed by this title shall be collected by the Bureau of Internal Revenue under the direction of the Secretary of the Treasury and shall be paid into the Treasury of the United States as internal- revenue collections. If the tax is not paid when due, there shall be added as part of the tax interest (except in the case of adjustments made in accordance with the provisions of sections 802 (b) and 805) at the rate of one-half of 1 per centum per month from the date the tax became due until paid.

(b) Such taxes shall be collected and paid in such manner, at such times, and under such conditions, not inconsistent with this title (either by making and filing returns, or by stamps, coupons, tickets, books, or other reasonable devices or methods necessary or helpful in securing a complete and proper collection and payment of the tax or in securing proper identification of the taxpayer), as may be prescribed by the Commissioner of Internal Revenue, with the approval of the Secretary of the Treasury.

(c) All provisions of law, including penalties, applicable with respect to any tax imposed by section 600 or section 800 of the Revenue Act of 1926 and the provisions of section 607 of the Revenue Act of 1934, shall, insofar as applicable and not inconsistent with the provisions of this title, be applicable with respect to the taxes imposed by this title.

(d) In the payment of any tax under this title a fractional part of a cent shall be disregarded unless it amounts to one-half cent or more, in which case it shall be increased to 1 cent.

SOCIAL SECURITY ACT OF 1935: TAXES WITH RESPECT TO EMPLOYMENT

RULES AND REGULATIONS

SEC. 808. The Commissioner of Internal Revenue, with the approval of the Secretary of the Treasury, shall make and publish rules and regulations for the enforcement of this title.

SALE OF STAMPS BY POSTMASTERS

SEC. 809. The Commissioner of Internal Revenue shall furnish to the Postmaster General without prepayment a suitable quantity of stamps, coupons, tickets, books, or other devices prescribed by the Commissioner under section 807 for the collection or payment of any tax imposed by this title, to be distributed to, and kept on sale by, all post offices of the first and second classes, and such post offices of the third and fourth classes as

(1) are located in county seats, or

(2) are certified by the Secretary of the Treasury to the Postmaster General as necessary to the proper administration of this title. The Postmaster General may require each such postmaster to furnish bond in such increased amount as he may from time to time determine, and each such postmaster shall deposit the receipts from the sale of such stamps, coupons, tickets, books, or other devices, to the credit of, and render accounts to, the Postmaster General at such times and in such form as the Postmaster General may by regulations prescribe. The Postmaster General shall at least once a month transfer to the Treasury, as internal- revenue collections all receipts so deposited together with a statement of the additional expenditures in the District of Columbia and elsewhere

SOCIAL SECURITY ACT OF 1935: TAXES WITH RESPECT TO EMPLOYMENT

incurred by the Post Office Department in performing the duties imposed upon said Department by this Act, and the Secretary of the Treasury is hereby authorized and directed to advance from time to time to the credit of the Post Office Department from appropriations made for the collection of the taxes imposed by this title, such sums as may be required for such additional expenditures incurred by the Post Office Department.

PENALTIES

SEC. 810.

(a) Whoever buys, sells, offers for sale, uses, transfers, takes or gives in exchange, or pledges or gives in pledge, except as authorized in this title or in regulations made pursuant thereto, any stamp, coupon, ticket, book, or other device, prescribed by the Commissioner of Internal Revenue under section 807 for the collection or payment of any tax imposed by this title, shall be fined not more than $1,000 or imprisoned for not more than six months, or both.

(b) Whoever, with intent to defraud, alters, forges, makes, or counterfeits any stamp, coupon, ticket, book, or other device prescribed by the Commissioner of Internal Revenue under section 807 for the collection or payment of any tax imposed by this title, or uses, sells, lends, or has in his possession any such altered, forged, or counterfeited stamp, coupon, ticket, book, or other device, or makes, uses, sells, or has in his possession any material in imitation of the material used in the manufacture of such stamp, coupon, ticket, book, or other device, shall be fined not more than $5,000 or imprisoned not more than five years, or both.

SOCIAL SECURITY ACT OF 1935: TAXES WITH RESPECT TO EMPLOYMENT

DEFINITIONS

SEC. 811. When used in this title-

(a) The term wages means all remuneration for employment, including the cash value of all remuneration paid in any medium other than cash; except that such term shall not include that part of the remuneration which, after remuneration equal to $3,000 has been paid to an individual by an employer with respect to employment during any calendar year, is paid to such individual by such employer with respect to employment during such calendar year.

(b) The term employment means any service, of whatever nature, performed within the United States by an employee for his employer, except-

   (1) Agricultural labor;

   (2) Domestic service in a private home;

   (3) Casual labor not in the course of the employer's trade or business;

   (4) Service performed by an individual who has attained the age of sixty-five;

   (5) Service performed as an officer or member of the crew of a vessel documented under the laws of the United States or of any foreign country;

   (6) Service performed in the employ of the United States Government or of an instrumentality of the United States;

SOCIAL SECURITY ACT OF 1935: TAXES WITH RESPECT TO EMPLOYMENT

(7) Service performed in the employ of a State, a political subdivision thereof, or an instrumentality of one or more States or political subdivisions;

(8) Service performed in the employ of a corporation, community chest, fund, or foundation, organized and operated exclusively for religious, charitable, scientific, literary, or educational purposes, or for the prevention of cruelty to children or animals, no part of the net earnings of which inures to the benefit of any private shareholder or individual."

STATE AND LOCAL EMPLOYEES

Employees who work for either a state or local governmental agency are sometimes not covered under Social Security. The reason for this is that often these workers have other benefits provided to them that those in private employment do not. When the Social Security Act was first initiated, these employees were not covered. It was later amended around 1991 when both state and local employers made an agreement with Social Security called "Section 218 agreements." This agreement extends Social Security benefits to those employed by either state or local agencies. Interestingly, SSA says this protection falls to the employment position rather than to a person. According to SSA, a person who is employed into a "position" that provides Social Security benefits should be made to pay into the benefits system. This is to provide public employees with the same access to Social Security benefits – the same that is provided to private employees. The way this happens is that state or local employees fall into two coverage groups. "Absolute coverage" is for employees who are not covered under the Social Security. Both law-enforcement and firefighter positions can fall under this category. Sometimes, they do not have access to the second of the two coverage groups known as "retirement coverage." This one is for those positions that are covered in a public retirement system.

THE WINDFALL ELIMINATION PROVISION

The Windfall Elimination Provision (WEP) is a Social Security law that reduces the amount of Social Security benefits that can be afforded to those who have other or additional means of retirement benefits. It is made to reduce unfair advantages of certain workers over others. This provision modifies the already existing SSA formula that calculates benefit amount for people who are not state or local employees. The main restriction is that you must have less than 30 years of coverage under Social Security to be eligible for this form of protection. Simply, if you get a pension from your state or local employer, this provision readjusts how your retirement or disability benefits are calculated.

GOVERNMENT PENSION OFFSET

According to *The Complete Idiot's Guide to Social Security and Medicare*, the Government Pension Offset law is designed to help "widows, or widowers who worked for federal, state or local government agencies in which they did not pay Social Security taxes." Typically, these types of employees are eligible for pension benefits that those in the private sector are not. This is similar to WEP as it was also designed to prevent "double dipping." This means a person can theoretically receive income from more than one source. While some people paid into Social Security taxes, others, like governmental employees could, up until a certain point, receive Social Security benefits when they had never paid into the system.

SECTION II: UNEMPLOYMENT COMPENSATION

Where Did It Come From?

There have been various types of unemployment insurance for years. Before the Social Security Act was first developed, unemployment was so rampant, the government decided to step in. By enabling unemployed workers to have a weekly compensation payment, legislators believed it would strengthen the economy. It did. By World War II, unemployment had decreased dramatically. Charged by the decrease in employment, the government developed the Employment Act of 1946. This said the federal government would generate policies to keep unemployment down and the economy strong. They essentially wanted to prevent another Great Depression.

SOCIAL SECURITY ACT OF 1935
TITLE III-GRANTS TO STATES FOR UNEMPLOYMENT COMPENSATION ADMINISTRATION

APPROPRIATION

SECTION 301. For the purpose of assisting the States in the administration of their unemployment compensation laws, there is hereby authorized to be appropriated, for the fiscal year ending June 30, 1936, the sum of $4,000,000, and for each fiscal year thereafter the sum of $49,000,000, to be used as hereinafter provided.

PAYMENTS TO STATES

SEC. 302. (a) The Board shall from time to time certify to the Secretary of the Treasury for payment to each State which has an unemployment compensation law approved by the Board under Title IX, such amounts as the Board determines to be necessary for the proper administration of such law during the fiscal year in which such payment is to be made. The Board s determination shall be based on

(1) the population of the State;

(2) an estimate of the number of persons covered by the State law and of the cost of proper administration of such law; and

(3) such other factors as the Board finds relevant. The Board shall not certify for payment under this section in any fiscal year a total amount in excess of the amount appropriated therefor for such fiscal year.

(b) Out of the sums appropriated therefor, the Secretary of the Treasury shall, upon receiving a certification under subsection

SOCIAL SECURITY ACT OF 1935
TITLE III-GRANTS TO STATES FOR UNEMPLOYMENT COMPENSATION ADMINISTRATION

(a), pay, through the Division of Disbursement of the Treasury Department and prior to audit or settlement by the General Accounting Office, to the State agency charged with the administration of such law the amount so certified.

PROVISIONS OF STATE LAWS

SEC. 303.

(a) The Board shall make no certification for payment to any State unless it finds that the law of such State, approved by the Board under Title IX, includes provisions for-

(1) Such methods of administration (other than those relating to selection,

tenure of office, and compensation of personnel) as are found by the Board to be reasonably calculated to insure full payment of unemployment compensation when due; and

(2) Payment of unemployment compensation solely through public employment offices in the State or such other agencies as the Board may approve; and

(3) Opportunity for a fair hearing, before an impartial tribunal, for all individuals whose claims for unemployment compensation are denied; and

(4) The payment of all money received in the unemployment fund of such State, immediately upon such receipt, to the Secretary of the Treasury to the credit of the Unemployment Trust Fund established by section 904; and

SOCIAL SECURITY ACT OF 1935
TITLE III-GRANTS TO STATES FOR UNEMPLOYMENT COMPENSATION ADMINISTRATION

(5) Expenditure of all money requisitioned by the State agency from the Unemployment Trust Fund, in the payment of unemployment compensation, exclusive of expenses of administration; an

(6) The making of such reports, in such form and containing such information, as the Board may from time to time require, and compliance with such provisions as the Board may from time to time find necessary to assure the correctness and verification of such reports; and

(7) Making available upon request to any agency of the United States charged with the administration of public works or assistance through public employment, the name, address, ordinary occupation, and employment status of each recipient of unemployment compensation, and a statement of such recipient s rights to further compensation under such law.

(b) Whenever the Board, after reasonable notice and opportunity for hearing to the State agency charged with the administration of the State law finds that in the administration of the law there is--

(1) a denial, in a substantial number of cases, of unemployment compensation to individuals entitled thereto under such law; or

(2) a failure to comply substantially with any provision specified in subsection (a); the Board shall notify such State agency that further payments will not be made to the State until the Board is satisfied that there is no longer any such denial or failure to comply. Until it is so satisfied it shall make no further certification to the Secretary of the Treasury with respect to such State."

What Is It?

Unemployment Compensation is financial protection afforded to people who have lost their jobs. After the Social Security Act was established, the federal government had the right to grant states money to provide an unemployment insurance trust fund. In 1939, the government collected both federal and state payroll taxes. This was established under the Federal Unemployment Tax Act.

How Does It Work?

The way this program is funded is that the government taxes business payrolls. Some of the costs can be offset by state contributions, as well. People who qualify for these types of benefits get about half of what they would receive if they were still employed. All U.S states have a limit as to how long a person can receive these benefits and offices may stop or extend payments, as they deem appropriate. The typical amount of time someone can receive unemployment compensation is for about 26 weeks. Some extended payments have been known to last for 39 weeks or even up to as much as 65 weeks, provided the circumstances are extenuating. The reason that unemployment insurance came about was to protect unemployed workers from prolonged hardship if they become involuntarily unemployed. In the beginning, only certain types of businesses could afford this protection, so many were left without help. The laws have since been adjusted.

Am I Eligible?

To qualify for unemployment compensation a person has to have worked for a covered employer. They also must have been employed for a specific duration and have earned a certain amount of money. In addition, people who want unemployment have to demonstrate a "willingness to seek and accept suitable employment." Different states have their own requirements about what it means to be "available" for work. But an unemployed worker must register with their local employment office, first. Know that if you get unemployment, you may be denied further benefits if, at some point, you refuse to accept a job offer. There are circumstances, according to federal law, that you may continue to receive unemployment compensation after refusing a reasonable job offer. For example, if a job opening exists, you may refuse to accept it, while receiving your benefits, if the vacancy is directly due to a "strike, lockout, or some other labor dispute." You may also refuse potential employment offer if the job is less favorable than other similar jobs in the same area. According to an excerpt from the *House of Ways and Means Greenbook* 2000, if "the wages, hours, or other conditions of the work are substantially less favorable to the individual than those prevailing for similar work in the locality," you may not be denied unemployment benefits. A person may also not be legally denied unemployment benefits if they get offered a job that as a condition of the employment would require a potential employee to join a labor union. Simply, you cannot get denied benefits if a potential employer tries to force you to join a labor group as a condition of the offer.

They Said "No." What Now?

According a recent Associated Press article, Tanja Shelton, a 35-year-old production control scheduler from Sioux Center, Iowa, was recently denied unemployment compensation. Shelton went through proper channels and her case ultimately came before administrative law judge, Lynette Donner. Judge Donner then denied Shelton's request for unemployment saying, "Ms. Shelton showed a willful and wanton disregard for the standard of behavior the employer has the right to expect for an employee." In an unrelated case, 26-year-old Emmalee Bauer was also denied unemployment compensation in the same week. The hotel clerk was fired for writing a journal on her computer.

So what is going on here? Why are these people being denied the right to benefits? An argument could be made that the administrative judge was assessing guilt to a potential claim when the question of guilt is not the question. The question is whether or not the worker broke regulations that govern unemployment, not what may or may not constitute "common sense."

Primarily, to better your chances of receiving unemployment, know the rules before something goes wrong. If you are denied, the first thing you should do is figure out whether or not you want to pursue the case. For the time and effort that is going to be involved, you might just want to find another job, if you can. Of course, you have the right to file an appeal, but how does one do this? Every state is different, but you will first get a denial notice in the mail from either an administrative examiner or deputy. Once you have received this, you have the right to file an appeal. For the most part, this appeal must be filed within a certain time of the initial denial – about two to four weeks. The time you have to appeal depends on where you live. For example, in Maine, a person must file an unemployment claim with the Department of Labor at the Division of Administrative Hearings.

SUMMARY

Chapter 5 covers:

What is an "employer?": According to the *Social Security Handbook*, you are defined as an "employer" if you "have the final authority or right to control workers in performing their services, including hiring, firing and supervising."

Employees should know: This section covers an employee's general responsibility about reporting his or her situation properly to SSA when he or she is hired at a job. An employer is required to give every new employee this piece of paper when he or she is first hired.

Employers should know: This section covers what an employer should do about reporting employee information to SSA. Typically, when an employer starts a business they get a Tax ID number from the government. An employer is also required to get all corresponding information from their employee (name, Social Security number, and so forth). They will need to enter this information on a W-2 form, otherwise known as a "Wage and Tax Statement," and submit this information appropriately.

Self-employed people should know: This section covers overall responsibilities for self-employed people regarding what to do when reporting to SSA. It also includes a portion about net earnings.

State and Local Employees: This section covers information about what Social Security benefits may be afforded to state and local employees.

Windfall Elimination Provision (WEP): A provision preventing federal, state, and local employees from having an unfair monetary advantage over employees in the private sector.

Government Pension Offset: A provision preventing widows and widowers, who were once governmental employees, from receiving too much money from retirement or "double-dipping" when they may not have had to pay into Social Security taxes when they were employed.

Unemployment Compensation: A way for unemployed workers to receive aid to help them get back into the workforce. This section has a general overview of factors that may qualify or disqualify a candidate from receiving money.

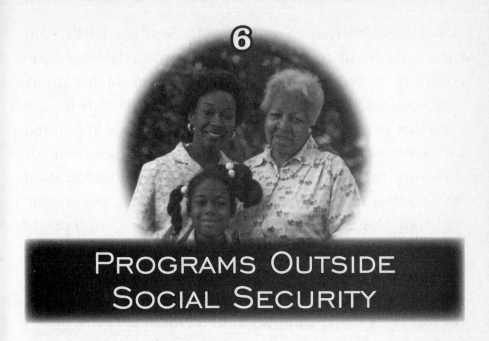

6

PROGRAMS OUTSIDE SOCIAL SECURITY

WHAT ARE THEY?

In many circumstances people do not qualify for Social Security and many assistance programs exist for this reason. Sometimes, people may find they may qualify eventually, but need extra time and help along the way – at least until that first benefit check, anyway. There are alternative programs out there that often have similar benefits to that of Social Security. This is not to suggest that people who do qualify for Social Security are not eligible. For whatever reason you may need assistance, know there are many federal, state and other local agencies that can help.

Federal

Just like the Social Security Administration, the U.S

Department of Health and Human Services (HHS) and the Department of Agriculture are two divisions of the government responsible for a wide range of programs and services. HHS, established in 1979, is run by the secretary of health and human services, who is appointed by the president and Congress. This section has 12 major divisions, the main of which is called "The Administration for Children and Families." This department is responsible for promoting quality care for children, youth, and needy families. Other important departments a person may need to know about are the Administration on Development Disabilities (ADD), Administration on Aging (AA), and the Office of Child Support Enforcement (CDE). The AA is the department that manages grants relating to the funding of state and local programs that have to do with older or elderly people. Medicare and Medicaid is an important one under this program, but I will talk about that in detail later in another chapter. The Department of Agriculture, originally a department within the Office of the Commissioner of Patents, also has many sections; one is responsible for food distribution nationwide. To find out any information about programs and services in your area, contact your local library. Some cities across the country have telephone referral emergency services. You may also be able to find valuable information by dialing "211" on your telephone.

Temporary Assistance for Needy Families (TANF)

Under HHS, the federal government had a program

called Aid for Families with Dependent Children (AFDC). It was originally established under the Social Security Act in 1935 and served as a cash benefit program for deprived children whose parents were absent from their home, unemployed, or deceased. The federal government mandated how states determined eligibility for this program; states were allowed a lot of latitude when establishing who was eligible and under what conditions. Abolished by President Bill Clinton, the program was later named "Temporary Assistance for Needy Families" (TANF) around the mid 1990s. As the name suggests, this program provides services much like AFDC did, only on a temporary basis and places work restrictions on those who receive benefits. TANF is designed to end a family's financial dependence on welfare by giving them an opportunity to participate in job training and various other employment assistance programs. To qualify in most states, a person has to have a low income, be a U.S. citizen, and be financially responsible for someone else who is under 19 years old.

Food Stamp Program & EBT

This program is designed for low-income individuals and families who need help buying food. Under this program, people may also qualify for assistance either supplementing or improving their diets. Years ago, participants were issued paper vouchers (that looked like monopoly money) that they could use to buy food at retail stores. Today, people who participate are issued electronic benefit transaction (EBT) cards that work like a debit card. Again, many states vary on how someone may be eligible, but to qualify you basically must:

- Not have a bank account, or combination of accounts, that exceed $2,001 and be responsible for someone who is 60 years old or younger or have a bank account, or combination of accounts, which exceed $3,001 and be responsible for someone who is 61 years old or older.

- Not have a household income that is over $11,677 if just one person lives in that residence.

- Not have a household income of more than $15,757 if two people live in the residence.

- Not have a household income of more than $19,849 if three people live in the residence.

- Not have a household income of more than $23,929 if four people live in the residence.

- Not have a household income of more than $29,009 if five people live in the residence.

- Not have a household income of more than $32,089 if six people live in the residence.

- Not have household income of more than $36,169 if seven people live in the residence.

- Not have a household income of more than $40,249 if more than seven people live in a residence.

Women, Infants, and Children (WIC)

The Woman, Infants, and Children (WIC) program is another assistance initiative designed to help low-income individuals or families. It is a nutritional supplemental food program run by governmental divisions within the Department of Agriculture. Infants and children up to 5 years old qualify, as well as pregnant or breastfeeding mothers. To be fully eligible, the main requirement is that either a mother or child will be at some nutritional- or medical-based risk without aid. A person has to be a U.S citizen and meet additional income requirements to qualify. Again, each state varies. There is also the WIC Farmer's Marker Nutrition program that helps families get fruits and vegetables.

Low-Income Home Energy Assistance

The HHS manages the low-income Home Energy Assistance program. It is another federally based assistance program that helps people pay their utility costs. Many states simply require that a person be of low-income, but some other restrictions can apply. For the most part, the main restriction is that a person's income fall between predetermined guidelines.

Emergency Food Assistance Program

The Emergency Food Assistance Program is federally funded and it helps low-income individuals, including the elderly, and families get food fast. All states within the United States have programs of this sort and one way to find out information is to call any local USDA in your region. Anyone can apply for assistance provided they can prove their circumstances are dire.

Child Support Enforcement (CSE)

In the early 1980s, the federal government made it mandatory that all states set up systems where child support orders could be enforced. The law is called the Child Support Enforcement Amendment of 1984. The main services these agencies now provide include DNA testing and help with locating absent parents. To qualify, you must be a caregiver in need of support service. Those who are already on some form of financial assistance, like TANF, for example, receive all services for free.

State

Assistance for Infants and Toddlers with Disabilities

This is a state run early intervention program for small children with disabilities. Eligibility requirements vary from state to state. If you have a child who is disabled and he or she is three years old or younger, you probably will qualify. Although most of these programs are free, some require a small or sliding-fee.

Special Milk Program

This program gives free milk to children, children's institutions, and other groups who do not participate in similar federally funded programs. Each state has its own eligibility requirements. Household income should not be more than $24,505 for a family of four. The Special Milk program is available for children at any age who may or may not participate in free/reduced school lunch programs.

Independent Services for Older and Blind Individuals

This program is for visually impaired people over 55 years old. It provides employment assistance for those who qualify. Requirements vary from state to state, but to be eligible, a person must be disabled. This program is also primarily geared toward people who have difficulty living on their own. Counseling is also a primary service available.

Local or Other

"Freedom From Hunger"

Originally called "Meals for Millions," this program provides information, resources, and food for anyone, anywhere in the world who needs it. It originated as the "brain child" of Clifford Clinton, a son of two missionaries, around the 1940s. It acts as a food cooperative between local communities. Today, with the Department of Agriculture, the program helps develop cooperatives globally. To find out where a program operates locally call: 1-800-708-2555.

Local Churches

Many local churches have food pantries, financial assistance, and referral services. The main eligibility requirement is that a person be in need, but you will probably have to have your Social Security number available as proof of ID. They also help with clothes, furniture, and other items. Churches often help people with referral services or educational and employment services free of charge.

The Salvation Army

A Salvation Army can be found pretty much anywhere in the United States. This organization provides various types of assistance in more than 97 countries worldwide. They have an innumerable amount programs. Some of them include: financial, food and housing, counseling, senior assistance, rehabilitation services, and various other social service programs.

FEDERAL, STATE, LOCAL, AND OTHER VALUABLE RESOURCES

There are many federal, state, local, and other online

resource services available to those who may or may not be eligible for Social Security benefits. The good news is that these services are free. You can get information about them from either your local library or from the privacy of your home. Some of these sites have eligibility "tool testers" to see if you can qualify for other programs and services, as well.

USA.gov

This is a federal Web site that has a lot of information about how to find out about services in your area. It has information about educational, employment, and social services. There is a section that tells you how to try and get unclaimed government money for free. It also gives information on how to get free childcare and other child service related information, medical insurance, rental assistance, and pension and insurance guaranties.

Prescription Help

A large percentage of Americans, including senior citizens, periodically have a lot of trouble affording their prescriptions. Often times, prescription assistance programs only help if you have "attempted to seek help elsewhere, but have not yet been able to secure said assistance." There is help for those who need it and criteria are not always based on whether you have received help somewhere else. It is not always contingent on whether or not you have Social Security or Medicare.

There are programs that can help everyone regardless of their circumstances. The trick is knowing where to look.

RxAssist

RxAssist, otherwise known as the "Patient Assistant Program Center," helps people find a way to get the prescriptions they need. They do not provide the assistance themselves, but they do have a vast amount of resources to direct you to those who can help. Sponsored by AstraZeneca, a major pharmaceutical company, RxAssist "offers a comprehensive database of these patient assistance programs, as well as practical tools, news, and articles so that health care professionals and patients can find the information they need. All in one place." For more information about this program or Rx Outreach, go online to **www.rxassist.org**.

Partnership for Prescription Assistance Program

According to Julie Theriault, president of the American Academy of Physician's Assistants, people from all walks of life have difficulty paying for their much-needed life-sustaining medications. She wrote, "More than one in five adults ages 18 to 64 was uninsured in 2003. More than eight out of ten people who are uninsured come from working families." More than 45 million people today remain uninsured and the numbers are rising everyday, according to the academy statistics.

The Partnership for Prescription Assistance program (PPA) is a national coalition of private organizations and companies, doctors, hospitals, and health-care associations all working to remedy what they feel is a growing national crisis. Suzanne Mintz, president of the National Family Caregivers Association said PPA also helps those with chronic illness. She said patients such as these often need large quantities of medications to simply survive. In a written testimonial, Ms. Mintz was quoted as saying, "Persons with chronic illnesses or disabilities tend to use more prescription medications than the average American. It is as if the Partnership for Prescription Assistance was designed with care giving families in mind. It fills a very big need. It is straight forward and simple to use – it will allow care giving families to quickly figure out what programs they are eligible for and apply for them." For more information about this program call 1-800-4PPA-NOW (1-800-477-2669) or go online to **www.pparx.org**.

SUMMARY

Chapter 6 covers:

Other Programs and Services: In many circumstances people do not qualify for Social Security; many assistance programs exist just for this reason. There are alternative programs that often have similar benefits to that of Social Security.

TANF: "Temporary Assistance for Needy Families" is a federal program that is designed to end a family's financial dependence on welfare (formerly known as AFDC) by giving them an opportunity to participate in job training and various other employment assistance programs. To qualify in most states, a person has to have a low-income, be a U.S. citizen, and be financially responsible for someone else who is under 19 years old.

Electronic Benefits Transfer: This program (formerly known as the "food stamp" program) is designed for low-income individuals and families who need help buying food. Under this program, people may also qualify for assistance either supplementing or improving their diets.

WIC: The "Women, Infants, and Children" program is another federal assistance initiative designed to help low-income individuals or families. It is a nutritional supplemental food program run by governmental divisions within the Department of Agriculture. Infants and children up to 5 years old qualify, as well as pregnant or breastfeeding mothers.

LIHEA: The Low-Income Home Energy Assistance program is managed by the Department of Health and Human Services and it is another federally based assistance program that helps people pay their utility costs.

EFAP: The Emergency Food Assistance Program is

federally funded and helps low-income individuals, including the elderly, and families get food fast.

CSE: Child Support Enforcement is part of a federal initiative developed in the 1980s that required all states set up systems where child support orders could be enforced.

AITD: Known as "Assistance for Infants and Toddlers with Disabilities," this is a state-run early intervention program for small children with disabilities.

ISOBI: The Independent Services for Older and Blind Individuals is a program for visually impaired people over 55 years old. It provides employment assistance and other similar benefits (like that provided under Social Security) for those who qualify.

"Celebrate the happiness that friends are always giving, make every day a holiday and celebrate just living!"

Amanda Bradley

7

SYSTEM IN DANGER

When people talk about Social Security, they often act as if they are dealing with an endangered species. But why? There are millions of dollars available, so what is the problem? Why do people on the news appear so scared?

The future of Social Security rests on the fact that the proportion of today's spending, almost one-fourth of the federal budget, is projected to increase dramatically. Medical and health care costs will also continue to increase. Some people believe that this, along with a rise in population and increased investments in private pensions and health plans, spells trouble. So what does this mean? It means the number of employed people paying into the system might decrease. When that happens, experts think the number of older people in the United States will more than double. Ever hear the term "Baby Boomers?" Because of their increased life expectancy, some say demand for money will rise. It has also been suggested that because of a sharp decrease in the birth rate (after the baby boomers) that less workers are born to pay later. Social Security will generate less money and filling the gap between less workers (less money coming in) and more beneficiaries (more need for money) is what presents a problem. Not for today, but eventually. When more people retire, less people are working and shelling out payroll taxes. Because of this, according to some, Social Security will generate less money and eventually go bankrupt. It is interesting to consider that people's fears may be the factor that will facilitate the insolvency.

Show Me the Money!

Rather than building up individual trusts funds for recipients, Social Security works as a "pay as you go" system. This means money that is paid to today's beneficiaries comes from today's workers. For example, if Joe has a job that takes Social Security taxes, his money goes to the 70-year-old retiree down the street, Mary. When she was employed, Mary's money went to beneficiaries of her day and so on. Because this system of payment has gone on for so long, there is plenty of money in reserve called a "surplus." Most experts project there will be a surplus for a while or at least it appears to be that way. Where does the money go in the mean time?

Well, the money is typically redirected to a pending fund called the "general revenue" fund. Basically, the government takes this money and spends it on whatever they want to. People often criticize the government for this kind of mismanagement. Sometimes, the government takes the Social Security money and spends it elsewhere. How this works is that the government sends the cash to the U.S. Treasury, who then issues bonds for it. The government then sells the bonds to whoever will buy them. Anyone. This is an involved way of borrowing money to pay your debts. You essentially spend money when you issue bonds, notes or securities, and so forth. If you were to spend too much money, you would run at a deficit. You cannot run at a deficit for too long, unless you are the U.S. government, that is.

So how is it that experts say that Social Security trust fund balances are at a surplus, when other "experts" say more money is spent than is taken in? Here is a basic example of how this might happen. Let us say Joe owed Mary some money. Joe then writes a note (IOU) to Mary promising to pay the money back. Joe now has a debt; Mary has an asset. In federal spending, Joe and Mary are the same person! Both the debt and asset belong to the same entity. After awhile, this money will not have the same value it did when it was generated. At some point in the future, the government will have to dip into the Treasury. After that, it is projected that Social Security will only be generating a portion of what it needs to keep up with demand – at only about 75 percent. It seems that no one is precisely sure, however.

WHAT IS A TRUST FUND?

A trust fund is a kind of bank account that is managed by one person for another. Commonly, these accounts can have interest shares that are paid to the person that it is set up for by a trustee. According to *The Complete Idiot's Guide to Social Security and Medicare*, "there are six trustees: the Secretary of the Treasury, the Secretary of Labor, the Secretary of Health and Human Services, the Commissioner of Social Security, and two members appointed by the president and confirmed by Senate to represent the public. They are John L. Palmer and Thomas Saving." As far as federal spending, there are three main types of Social Security and Medicare trust funds. The Old Age and Survivors Insurance Trust Fund (OASI) is a fund that incorporates monies that have to do with retirement and survivor benefits. The Disability Insurance fund (DI) pays disability benefits. Hospital trust fund (HI) is the portion of the trust fund that pays for Medicare Part A. The Supplementary Medicare Insurance trust (SMI) covers Part B of Medicare, but this part is not paid for via Social Security and Medicare payroll taxes. The federal government trust funds work in a similar way, and the government must invest the money from them in "interest bearing securities that are guaranteed by the U.S. Government." They are also not attachable. That means in the event the account holder goes bankrupt, no lien can be placed against the value of the money in the trust fund. So, Social Security uses Treasury bonds backed up by something called the "full faith and credit" of the government. What does this mean? The "full faith and credit" is a clause (Article IV Sec. 1) in the Constitution that acts like a gentleman's promise. Conveniently, the clause means when the government owes money, they will use all their power (taxing, borrowing, or other means) to pay their debts back. The constitutional clause reads as follows:

> Full Faith and Credit shall be given in each State to the public Acts, Records, and judicial Proceedings of every other State. And the Congress may by general Laws prescribe the Manner in which such Acts, Records, and Proceedings shall be proved, and the Effect thereof.

What Now?

Because of all the projected difficulty, the government is trying to devise a way to keep the money flowing. It will be difficult for future workers for a couple of reasons. Resources the system has today are promised, according to President Bush, to today's and near retirees. It is interesting that Bush uses the phrase "promised." Remember Flemming v. Nestor? The Supreme Court case decision said Social Security was not guaranteed to anyone, but was a matter of condition. So what does that means for people who have not entered the workforce? In all likelihood, they are going to have to "foot the bill" for any future reforms that will inevitably come. So, what changes are coming?

REFORMS

To fix Social Security, the government will probably raise payroll taxes or raise the cap on the amount of income to be taxed – remember the increase from $97,500 to $102,000. Experts project that the retirement age will be increased and benefits will be decreased. Some officials want to dip into the government's general revenue fund. This would cause the national deficit to rise. A "deficit" is the difference between government expenditures and tax revenues. This deficit is also fed by government borrowing. Issuing bonds is one way they borrow money. Another possible reform on the horizon is changing the way the cost of living is adjusted. Remember, the cost of living adjustment or "COLA" is defined as the amount of money that is needed to goods and services you need. This is determined by the Consumer Price Index (CPI), which measures overall changes in prices over time. This would mean possibly reducing the standard of living because the price of things you want to buy typically goes up, not down.

MORE ON PRIVATIZATION

Back to privatization. President Bush says he wants to take a portion of a worker's taxable income obligation (your Social Security taxes), and invest it into something called "diversified portfolios." When you retire, the amount of benefits you could receive is possibly reduced. Rather than give benefits in accordance with the amount you have paid into Social Security, your benefits might be contingent on how well the market does or does not perform. This is a matter of concern for a lot of people. The cost of this idea may be too much to bear. Proponents of privatization say that if monies are invested, the return is going to be greater, but this is not true in every circumstance. Conceivably, a person could pay less Social Security tax, and get more later when the time comes to receive benefits. But you do not always get what you pay for. Most experts agree that having personal accounts in this manner will not ensure that Social Security remains strong, secured, or "solvent." Additionally, readjusting how benefits are calculated will, in all likelihood, amount to less benefits and services in the end. Today, the question that some people are asking is "Whose money is it anyway?" They ask, "Should not the money people pay over the many years of their work lifetime be earmarked for them or their children?" If everyone paid his or her social insurance tax toward that end, would there be a steady base of money later? Privatizing Social Security may create an unfair advantage and a bigger "base" for certain people. It also seemingly rejects the ideals (remember Townsend and Roosevelt) to which is was originally intended – to help those who spent a lifetime working, but for whatever reason, can no longer help themselves.

WHAT CAN I DO ABOUT IT?

A lot of people have no idea, for the most part, how to navigate the maze of Social Security reforms that might be coming. The task appears daunting, to say the least. One thing a person can do is to find out information from an advocacy group that they are interested in, but be careful. Sometimes, advocacy groups are more wrapped up in a cause than they are with the people the cause should be helping; they can be a valuable ally, however. People who are part of these advocacy communities feel deeply about the subject matter they are entrenched in. Learn from them and listen if you want to become involved in securing the future of Social Security.

SUMMARY

Chapter 7 covers:

System in danger: The future of Social Security rests on the fact that the proportion of today's spending, almost one-fourth of the federal budget, is projected to increase dramatically. Medical and health care costs will also continue to increase.

Pay as you go: Rather than building up individual trusts funds for recipients, Social Security works as a "pay as you go" system. This means the money paid to today's beneficiaries comes from today's workers.

What is a Trust Fund?: A trust fund is a kind of bank account that is managed by one person for another. Commonly, these accounts can have interest shares that are paid to the person that it is set up for by a trustee.

OASI Trust Fund: The Old Age and Survivors Insurance Trust Fund (OASI) is a fund that incorporates monies that have to do with retirement and survivor benefits. It is one of three major types of Social Security trust funds.

DI Trust Fund: The Disability Insurance fund (DI) pays disability benefits. It is another type of Social Security trust fund.

HI Trust Fund: Hospital Trust Fund (HI) is the portion of the trust fund that pays for Medicare Part A.

SMI Trust Fund: The Supplementary Medicare Insurance trust (SMI) covers Part B of Medicare, but this part is not paid for via Social Security and Medicare payroll taxes.

Full faith and credit: This a clause (Article IV Sec. 1) in the Constitution that says the government will use their power (taxing, borrowing, or other means) to pay their debts back.

"Happiness comes of the capacity to feel deeply, to enjoy simply, to think freely, to risk life, to be needed."

Storm Jameson

HELP! I HAVE BEEN DENIED

Imagine that you have applied for Social Security benefits, but have been denied. What could you do about it? What if you have already been receiving benefits and then had them taken away? Who would you call? There are a number of things a person can do in these circumstances, but sometimes they may not be aware of how to help themselves. Do you know what cessation means? Your local Social Security examiner is required to send you a status letter (decision notice) if or when something in your case changes. They will not concern themselves, however, as to whether or not you know what the information they send you means. So, before I talk about more administrative stuff, let us start with some useful tips in the event a problem arises.

WHO DENIES CLAIMS?

Typically, the person reviewing your case will be a "claims

examiner." This person is involved with disability cases. The two types are an "initial claims examiner" and a "reconsideration examiner." The first is the person who gets your information when you first file a claim. The second reviews the work done by the first examiner. It is kind of a "checks and balances" system or at least it is supposed to be.

There are safeguards in place, however, that should catch these individuals who may over extend their authority. Supervisors and managers, if they are doing their job properly, can stop a case from being arbitrarily denied. But if no one is paying attention, this could spell trouble, for you that is. Obviously, some examiners are meticulous and do their jobs properly. Others are simply lazy and try to get your paperwork completed without real thought to what they are doing. According to Nolo, there are ways you can preempt their haphazard approach. First, make it a priority to speak with your examiner over the telephone. If they appear to be evasive or unable to answer your questions, make them explain everything to you in detail. When I was a reporter, my editor told me to take the "Colombo" approach with people who did no simply want to take the time to deal with me during an interview. It means just acting unclear about a topic. The examiner may be curt or even try to dissuade you from asking questions by behaving as if they do not simply "have the time" to answer your questions. You have the right to have your case explained to your satisfaction. The best thing is to be polite as possible and stay on that telephone until you are perfectly clear about what you want to know. If for some reason they ask, "Can I call you back?" there is a high probability they are not going to call you back, so stay on the telephone.

One more thing to watch out for, according to Nolo, is to make sure the claims examiner does not give you misinformation. For example, if you know a decision was made without sufficient medical information, that may be a problem. The reason is that it is against the law for the examiner to make certain decisions without checking with someone else first, mainly a qualified medical consultant. They may simply try to avoid doing this to save themselves from extra work. Often times, claims examiners believe they are so experienced at their job, they do not need to follow certain disability protocols. Again, try to make a concerted effort to have a little information about the system and how it works ahead of time. It may save you from some serious heartache later.

WHAT IS AN APPEAL?

The first thing you should do in the event your case is denied is to file an initial appeal. This could be said about any claims you make with Social Security. An appeal is made when you want to challenge a decision that has been made on your case. If you are denied, you have a limited amount of time to respond with an appeal. Notices should have e-mails or telephones numbers that you may call.

WHO IS AN ADMINISTRATIVE LAW JUDGE?

After a person has filed an initial appeal, a secondary "hearing process" begins. The next step will probably involve going before an Administrative Law Judge (ALJ). According to SSA, this is a person who will make an "independent decision based on evidence" held. The ALJ is a federal judge who hears cases at the first step of an appeal, but do not think their decisions are entirely based independently of your claims examiner. The examiner will have the "ear" of the judge when you, in all likelihood, will not. To optimize your chances of being equally heard, remember to document any communication and correspondence that you have had with anyone from Social Security. It is important that you try and get those documents to the ALJ before the hearing takes place. After you get a hearing with the ALJ, SSA says they will send you notification of where and when you need to show up. This happens in about 20 days. There can be delays due to "the volume of pending appeals or delays due to ALJ travel schedules."

What Is with All the Technical Jargon?

Typically, a claims examiner will talk with you over the phone about details of your case. Unfortunately, he or she can use technical jargon that is very confusing. People do not like to feel stupid, so they sometimes do not ask questions for fear of embarrassment. An examiner might do this on purpose to dissuade you from questioning his or her authority. Make sure if you are unclear in any way, to stop and ask them, "What is with all the technical jargon?" Here are a few terms you may come across:

Body System: SSA uses this term to refer to "illnesses and impairments by body systems." For example, if you had a heart condition, SSA would probably categories it under a cardiovascular category. If you have epilepsy, this would be placed under the "neurology" category. SSA has a list of typical disorders or illness that are common.

WHAT IS CESSATION?

The term comes from the Latin word "cessare" meaning to "hold back." As far as Social Security is concerned, this term is a fancy way of saying you will not get benefits anymore. There are various types of cessations, but they all mean the same thing. Again, you can challenge a cessation by either filing a request for reconsideration (recon) or by filing an appeal.

WHAT IS A MEDICAL SOURCE STATEMENT?

According to the SSA, a Medical Source Statement is an acceptable medical source's opinion on your ability, despite any impairment(s), to do work-related activities such as sitting, standing, walking, lifting, carrying, handling objects, hearing, speaking, and traveling.

SUMMARY

Chapter 8 covers:

Who denies claims?: The person who will deny your claim will be a "claims examiner." This person is involved with disability cases. The two types are an "initial claims examiner" and a "reconsideration examiner."

Appeal: An appeal is made when you want to challenge a decision that has been made on your case. If you are denied, know that you have a limited amount of time to respond with an appeal.

Administrative Law Judge: According to SSA, this is a person that will make an "independent decision based on evidence" held. The ALJ is a federal judge who hears cases at the first step of an initial appeal.

Cessation: The term comes from the Latin word "cessare" meaning to "hold back." As far as Social Security goes, it means all or an element of your case will be stopped.

Medical Source Statements: According to *How to Get SSI and Social Security Disability*, a Medical Source Statement (MSS), "is the opinion of a licensed medical practitioner that details what, if any, limitations the claimant's impairments impose on his ability to perform work or work-like activities; or stated positively, what the claimant is able to do despite his impairments."

INSIGHT FROM THE PROFESSIONALS

Many different Social Security advocacy groups, governmental organizations, and other entities and "think-tanks" have conducted various case studies about Social Security. Issues such as privatization, poverty, and solvency (or insolvency, depending on your perspective) have long been the "hot-bed" of political debate. When I first received the assignment to write this book, my editor told me that I would need to incorporate a batch of case studies. Coming from graduate school, I did not think anything of it at the time, but thinking back, I should have known better than to agree as the task has proved to be daunting, to say the least. As the subject of Social Security is so broad, it was difficult narrowing down what information is most relevant. In an effort to remain consistent, I simply tried to align the subject matter with information already presented in previous chapters. Below are some examples of case studies conducted over the past two decades.

WHAT IS A CASE STUDY?

A case study is a way of determining two things: a problem and a solution to that problem – usually in that order. A lot of times, people in business or government approach case studies as a kind of puzzle that needs to be solved. The puzzle is a way to get where you are going, a journey, if you will. The solution should come at the end of your approach or puzzle. If you did it right, that is. Social scientists, statisticians, and even some project management personnel often mistakenly formulate a study result before they actually delineate a problem to begin with. In this circumstance, the "puzzle" gets adjusted a little in reverse. Know that results from case studies conducted backwards may appear polluted. This will dramatically inhibit the ability to find clear-cut solutions.

SECTION I: A CASE STUDY IN PRIVATIZATION

As stated earlier, privatization means "to transfer to private ownership an economic enterprise or public utility that has been under state ownership." Privatization is generally initiated by businesses or governmental bodies to improve overall services and generate more money for systems that are lacking or in peril – in this case, the system of Social Security. Proponents of privatization believe transferring ownership of Social Security "enterprise" to the private sector is a way to increase systems efficiency and ensure solvency (the ability to pay all debts – under the current system of Social Security some say the program will run out of money in virtually decades). They believe it may also relieve the pension burden on the national budget. Opponents, however, believe the transfer may cause more problems than it will solve. It may cause added burden to low-wage workers and increase social disparity (or "class struggle"). Some say privatization will also steer Social Security away from the "social consciousness" ideals for which it was originally intended. Remember, Social Security was brought about to help people who cannot help themselves. Privatization mainly is concerned with optimizing money gains, not caring for the elderly, infirmed or disabled, for example. One way to examine the effectiveness of privatization is to look at how successful the concept is elsewhere.

CASE STUDY: CENTER FOR RETIREMENT RESEARCH

In a case study conducted by the Center for Retirement Research at Boston College (CRRW), John B. Williamson, a professor of Sociology, said that people should be careful when examining both successes and failures of privatization between countries whose demographics may vary dramatically.

CASE STUDY: CENTER FOR RETIREMENT RESEARCH

He said the impact of privatization has the potential to vastly improve the interests of people across the country, but careful scrutiny is warranted.

> "While developments in Chile offer a number of potential insights relevant to the privatization debate in the United States, Chile differs from the United States in many ways including population, level of economic development, social structure, and cultural background. Such differences limit the value of the Chilean experience as a source of information about what would happen were the United States to privatize its Social Security system." (Williamson, 3).

Mr. Williamson said countries like Sweden and Australia have had some success with partial privatization. He said that among the industrialized nations, however, the United Kingdom is most culturally similar to the United States and may serve as the best privatization "policy" model.

> "There are many reasons that Britain is relevant as a policy model for the United States. One is that it has more than ten years of experience with pension policy reforms similar to those currently being considered by American policy makers. While the evidence is not all in with respect to the long-term affects of recent privatization British reforms, preliminary evidence is available with respect to some potential strengths and problems. Another reason for taking a close look at this case is that Britain is in many ways structurally and culturally similar to the United States. In both countries, discourse (a discussion of a subject matter through speech or writing),

CASE STUDY: CENTER FOR RETIREMENT RESEARCH

about Social Security is dominated by a repositioned center-left and neo-liberalism. Britain has many of the same powerful interest groups and a very similar set of social values including those emphasizing the importance of freedom, autonomy and individual self-help. Given that Britain has an older age structure than does the United States, it provides a glimpse of the demographic pressure the U.S. will be facing several years from now" (Williamson, 8).

GRADUATED PENSIONS

In the 1960s, the United Kingdom initiated legislation to partially privatize its national pension system. "Graduated pensions" were contributions into the British National Insurance program, which mandated that payments were made based on a person's income. Monies were then sectioned into "units" that had their own value worth a predetermined amount. According to the CRRW study, these pensions were supposed to alleviate any burden (or payment increases) felt by employers who already had to pay into existing insurance systems. The study showed that under this premise, employers were under little or no pressure to increase benefits at any time. The government then decided to replace the graduated pension system with the State Earnings Related Pension System (SERPS). The program ran successfully for 24 years. Services were then extended by the State Second Pension in April 2002. It provided additional protection to low-income wage earners.

STAKEHOLDER PENSIONS

In the United Kingdom, a stakeholder pension works similar to that of a personal pension plan. They are mainly targeted for people who do not have an occupational (or work-related) pension scheme from their place of employment. This enables people to develop a retirement plan for themselves and their families. The main problem with this program is that these types of pension benefits are not guaranteed. As with any investment, the value of the fund may be contingent on investment performance – meaning the return on an investment paid fluctuates periodically. One could conceivably pay money for a lifetime and then get nothing in return.

SOCIAL SECURITY IN THAILAND

According to a study conducted by the United Nations International Labor Organization, Thailand's Social Security system will be bankrupt by 2051. The organization said the current system will collapse in 45 years if the country does not "adopt a national pension fund to boost savings." The study also concluded Thailand has no administrative methodology in place to ensure continued employer and employee contributions in the system. A similar study conducted by the Asian Development Bank (ADB) concurred with the UN findings. In 2006, the ADB told Thailand's Finance Ministry that contributions to Social Security funds will be mandatory as soon as 2018. Director-general Naris Chaiyasoot said employers and employees should begin contributing into the pension fund equally to the tune of approximately 6 percent.

The ADB estimates if the pension fund is eventually successful, it will generate nearly 80 billion baht per year (Baht = approximately .031945 U.S. dollars).

CASE STUDY: THE "PROS" OF U.S. PRIVATIZATION

According to a case study conducted by the Federal Reserve Bank of Cleveland's former senior economic advisor, Jagadeesh Gokhale, privatization will enable everyone, low-income wage earners in particular, to save for their retirement safely. He said investing a portion of Social Security taxes into individualized accounts will generate more "bequeathable" wealth to participants and remedy what he termed as an "inequality of wealth distribution in America" (Gokhale, 2).

"Poor households currently save very little and therefore own almost no financial wealth at retirement. As a result, the distribution of bequeathable wealth among retirees in the United States is highly unequal. There is strong evidence that Social Security may be contributing to that inequality. In contrast, a system of individual accounts would allow workers to accumulate real bequeathable wealth, leading ultimately to greater overall equality of wealth. Social Security privatization therefore becomes the truly progressive option for reform" (Gokhale, 1).

CASE STUDY: THE "PROS" OF U.S. PRIVATIZATION

According the study, individual accounts could reduce the need to increase tax rates or cut Social Security benefits. Additionally, accumulating wealth could compensate for any future changes or reductions to government benefits that "Congress deemed necessary to balance the system."

Source: **http://www.cato.org/pubs/ssps/ssp23.pdf** Reprinted with Permission from Jagadeesh Gokhale.

According to a study conducted by Employee Benefit Research Institute (EBRI), a non-profit, nonpartisan research organization, lower income workers may be able to receive higher levels of Social Security benefits under an individual accounts plan as proposed by President Bush. The data suggests, however that people should take caution as benefits level may fluctuate dramatically.

"For someone 20 years old today (born in 1985) also earning $16,500 a year, Social Security benefits under current law would be $12,500 at age 65. Because this person will reach normal retirement age after the date when Social Security's revenues will fall below its costs, benefits would be cut sharply, to $7,700 a year. By contrast, if policymakers decided to cut benefits gradually over time, annual Social Security payments would be $9,800. Under Model 2, the individual account plan, annual Social Security benefits would range from $10,800 to $15,700, depending on how the account assets were invested."

The EBRI study also conducted research on how individual accounts could affect older citizens with higher income levels. According to EBRI's director of Social Security Reform Research, the study also incorporated data on how individual accounts may affect those

CASE STUDY: THE "PROS" OF U.S. PRIVATIZATION

people who have yet to be born. In both aforementioned scenarios, they data suggests that those individuals, 50 years old or older, who make $72,000 a year or more, would receive more than $23,000 annually upon retirement. A person born in 2015, according to the research, earning an average of $55,000 annually, could expect $36,500 in annual Social Security benefits. Again, benefits would still vary slightly as the research is assuming laws or dollar value remains constant.

For <<those>> 50 or older, payments would be the same if policymakers waited for the Trust Fund shortfall to hit and then cut benefits. Under the gradual reduction of benefits option, the annual Social Security payment would be $22,900. Those not yet born, that benefit would be $22,700 under the option of waiting until the Trust Fund is exhausted and then cutting benefits sharply. Cutting benefits gradually over time would leave benefits of $24,500 a year.

CASE STUDY: OPPONENTS OF PRIVATIZATION

According to a case study conducted at the Department of Political Science at Yale University by associate professor Jacob Hacker, the government may have an ulterior motive to privatizing Social Security.

He said privatization may simply be a way to hand over money control to "private actors" who are not bound by the same regulations as governmental entities — meaning private businesses are allowed to behave in ways that government is not due to restrictive regulations.

CASE STUDY: OPPONENTS OF PRIVATIZATION

"The privatization agenda in social policy encompasses four main priorities: (1) the scaling back of direct government action to encourage self-reliance and private provision; (2), the expansion of subsidies for private insurance, savings, and charitable activities; (3), the expansion of government contracting with voluntary organizations and for-profit service providers; and (4), the infusion into established programs of vouchers and other mechanisms that allow [or require] recipients to opt out of these programs and obtain benefits from the private sector instead. None of these strategies eliminates government's role. Rather, they shift the emphasis from direct state action to the management and oversight of private actors operating within a new regulatory framework" (Hacker 5).

Source: www.law.yale.edu/documents/pdf/Hacker_PoliticsOfRisk Privatization.pdf

SECTION II: A STUDY IN POVERTY

A case study conducted at the National Academy for Social Insurance (NASI) found that more than half of the nation's Social Security recipients live below the poverty line. According to the data, more than 60 percent of the beneficiaries are elderly widows.

Both policy analyst Christina Smith FitzPatrick and vice president and director of Family Economic Security at NASI, Joan Entmacher, said that any "knee-jerk" or haphazard attempt by the U.S. government to reform

Social Security will only cause the numbers to rise. They also said one effective solution to help the "economically vulnerable" would entail raising Survivor benefits proportionally.

During an August 2000 NASI conference, both Ms. FitzPatrick and Ms. Entmacher presented their case study brief delineating various options that could better facilitate effective change in Social Security, thereby ensuring economic protection for the poverty stricken.

The Center for Budget Policy Priorities (CBPP), a nonpartisan research organization, conducted a national study on how Social Security affects poverty in America. According to the Associated Press, study results released from CBPP suggested that a large portion of both senior and elderly Americans could not sustain themselves financially without benefits. The data suggested that although SSA programs do, in fact, help some in need, a disproportionate amount of citizens are still left unprotected.

Dan Mitchell, a researcher from the Heritage Foundation (a conservative "think-tank"), said the case study was badly timed and inconclusive. He said the center often routinely conducts case studies of ongoing problems, as well. "It's sort of interesting that people are putting out studies when there isn't a plan yet," Mitchell said.

CASE STUDY: "OLD IN AMERICA"

A study conducted by the Progressive Policy Institute (PPI), said there will be difficulty ensuring the longevity of Social Security. According to the institute's president, Will Marshall, the problems are mainly due to too much governmental borrowing and partisan politics. He said if something is not done soon, apathy will turn what is currently a manageable problem into "full-blow national crisis."

"In truth neither side is willing to embrace the politically difficult steps necessary to assure Social Security's long-term solvency" (**http://www.ppionline.org/documents/Marshall_Soc_Sec_Chapter.pdf, page 50**).

CASE STUDY: THE FUTURE OF SOCIAL SECURITY RESTS WITH EDUCATION

According to the Academy of Economic and Financial Experts, education is the key to ensuring the stability of Social Security. Gary Anderson and James Keys, both instructors at the Florida International University's College of Business, said education is one way to increase individual income. By bolstering community potential, individuals can fuel overall economic earning capacity.

"The contribution education makes to a society is eloquently expressed by the philosopher Diogenes Laertius, 'The

CASE STUDY: THE FUTURE OF SOCIAL SECURITY RESTS WITH EDUCATION

foundation of every state is the education of its youth.' Similarly, philosophers have identified education as an instrumental variable in building human capital. Aristotle and Plato, respectively, observed that 'Education is the best provision for old age' and 'The direction in which education starts a man will determine his future.'"

CURRENT TRENDS

Many Americans are concerned how the future of Social Security will fair in concert with the skyrocketing national deficit. Questions about insolvency and Social Security reform are two topics that consistently seem to be on people's minds. It is still difficult to gauge, however, how the public thinks about the issues overall. Admittedly, even the most accurate data may exclude people who have no voice.

According to a public poll conducted by the American Association of Retired Persons (AARP), an overwhelming percentage of people, age 42 and up, strongly opposed privatization. Rather than implement new overall legislation, they said the government needs to work with the programs already in place.

Seven in ten respondents oppose private accounts (72 percent). The percentage of respondents who strongly opposed private accounts (58 percent) is seven times greater than those who strongly support (8 percent) private accounts.

In contrast, researchers at the National Center for Policy Analysis, said that people are in favor of privatization and that it is a proactive way to fix problems with Social Security. According to their information, the current system of Social Security is beyond repair.

Rather than go back and forth between a conglomerate of resources, the Gallup Organization conducted its own research. In a series of nation-wide polls, people were asked if whether or not they believe the Social Security system to be in peril. Although most people said that the program has major problems, they believe there is no impending "crisis" at all.

CIVIL RIGHTS COMMISSION AND SOCIAL SECURITY

Because of growing concern over the future of Social Security, the U.S. Commission on Civil Rights proposed two case studies to Congress about how the current system may adversely affect minority populations nationwide. In response, members of Congress wrote a letter to the U.S. Commission on Civil Rights (UCCR) chastising them for conducting "biased" case studies and misappropriating governmental resources. Congress also detailed in the letter how "blacks are afforded a disproportionate level of Social Security survivor and disability benefits." Congress did not address the issue of how more disaffected minorities in America die or become disabled from medically preventable diseases.

THE LETTER DATED MARCH 16, 2005, WAS ADDRESSED TO THE COMMISSION CHAIRMAN AND READS AS FOLLOWS:

March 16, 2005

The Honorable Gerald A. Reynolds

Dear Mr. Chairman:

We recently obtained documents indicating that the independent U.S. Commission on Civil Rights is preparing to enter the debate over the future of Social Security. [1]

The documents indicate that at its March 18 meeting, the Commission will consider two proposed studies on Social Security. [2] The first is a proposed Office of Civil Rights evaluation entitled, Building an Ownership Society: The Impact of Social Security Reform on Minorities. The second proposal is for an Office of General Counsel "legal analysis of any race-conscious elements of proposed Social Security reforms." [3]

We have serious reservations about whether these studies are an appropriate use of the Commission's limited funds.

The primary goals of the Commission on Civil Rights are "to investigate complaints alleging that citizens are being deprived of their right to vote" and "to study and collect information relating to discrimination or a denial of equal protection." The proposal to study Social Security does not appear related to these goals. In fact, the Office of Civil Rights proposal acknowledges this directly, stating

THE LETTER DATED MARCH 16, 2005, WAS ADDRESSED TO THE COMMISSION CHAIRMAN AND READS AS FOLLOWS:

that the study does "not fulfill USCCR standards" and is not directly related to the "mission statement nor to strategic plan goals. [4]

The role of the Commission is to ensure that all Americans have equal rights, not to produce politically biased reports in support of President Bush's Social Security privatization proposal. In light of these concerns, we ask that you respond to the following questions about these proposals by March 25:

1. Is consideration of Social Security consistent with the statutory mandate of the Commission? If so, why do the Commission documents note that the studies do "not fulfill USCCR standards for a statutory report," and are "not directly related to the USCCR mission statement."

2. Have USCCR Commissioners or staff had any contact with staff from the White House or other executive branch offices regarding these studies? If so please provide a list of all contacts, including relevant documents detailing the content of these contacts.

3. Have USCCR Commissioners or staff had any contact with staff from outside organizations, such as the Heritage Foundation, the Cato Institute, or Americans for Tax Reform regarding these studies? If so, please provide a list of all contacts, including relevant documents detailing the content of these contacts.

4. What is the anticipated budget for these proposed studies? Has the Commission traditionally conducted studies that do "not fulfill USCCR standards for a statutory report," and are "not directly related to the USCCR mission statement"? If so,

THE LETTER DATED MARCH 16, 2005, WAS ADDRESSED TO THE COMMISSION CHAIRMAN AND READS AS FOLLOWS:

please provide a list of these reports, as well as a discussion of the amount of the USCCR budget that was spent on these studies.

Thank you for your response to this request.

Sincerely,

Nancy Pelosi

Henry A. Waxman John Conyers, Jr.

Democratic Leader Ranking Minority Member Ranking Minority Member

Committee on Government Committee on the Judiciary

Reform

Charles B. Rangel, Sander M. Levin, Rosa L. DeLauro

Ranking Minority Member, Member of Congress, Member of Congress

Committee on Ways and Means

Xavier Becerra Grace F. Napolitano

Chair Chair

Congressional Hispanic Caucus Congressional Hispanic Caucus

Social Security Task Force

Source: http://oversight.house.gov/documents/20050316184239-96199.pdf

OBESITY AND SOCIAL SECURITY DISABILITY

A study issued by *The Lancet* (a weekly medical journal in the United Kingdom) said experts believe there may be a correlation between increases in Social Security Disability claims and obesity. The Social Security Administration concurred with the study findings and said that more than 77 million people are now paid monthly due to obesity and other related health problems. According to the American Obesity Association, Social Security regulators have attempted to make it more difficult for those who consider themselves "disabled" by obesity or other related health problems to claim disability assistance. In concert with this, a Harvard medical study conducted last year suggested that "only a mix of public and private solutions will change fundamental patterns of behavior" that lead to obesity.

WOMEN AND SOCIAL SECURITY

A study issued by the Women's Institute for Secure Retirement (WISER), a national nonprofit organization for women, said women face unique challenges in dealing with their retirement. It revealed that women generally live longer than men and must learn to plan accordingly – meaning they must plan for longer retirement with less money. Because of their social placement as primary caregivers, which is not recognized as viable or even economically contributory, according to the study, women spend more time out of the workforce, are more likely to work part-time jobs with little or no benefits and generally earn less overall. The study estimated that among newly retired, women average approximately 13 years of "zero" since the age of 22.

> *This is on average 13 fewer years to earn a pension if one is even available; 13 fewer years to climb the ladder toward better jobs and better pay; and 13 fewer years to put money away through a defined contribution plan or IRA. Every time a career is interrupted, the ladder toward better jobs and better pay must be re-established when a woman rejoins the labor force. She loses not only time but often must start over after taking time off.*

Source: **http://www.wiserwomen.org/pdf_files/sena tetestimony_final.pdf**

Because of structural barriers within Social Security, WISER Executive Director Cindy Hounsell said women rely too heavily on benefits payments that may relegate them below poverty levels – more so than their male counterparts.

The study was presented to Congress during a Capitol Hill hearing in March 2006. Director Hounsell told Congress a way to remedy any potential financial difficulty is to educate women about their circumstances and their financial futures.

SOCIAL SECURITY REFORM AND WOMEN

According to a global study conducted by the National Center for Policy Analysis (NCPA), a non-profit public policy research institute (favoring private sector solutions), women will have much to gain by Social Security reform – with individual accounts, in particular. The study examined the experiences of women in countries with already existing pension reforms in Argentina, Chile and Mexico in contrast to the U.S Social Security system. It compared both men and women's relative position with similar education and found that with monies generated from individual accounts, public benefits geared toward lower income earners and joint pensions, women were able to secure a far greater level of financial security than they could without any Social Security reforms. It has been, according to the study, a long standing debate as to whether or not women would be ill affected by Social Security reform. Many experts believed that a "status quo" would be the best way to help women overall.

The total pensions of women in these countries come from three sources: personal accounts, public benefits that are targeted toward low earners, and joint pensions that husbands are required to provide. In all three countries, husbands are required to purchase, with the money in their personal accounts, a joint annuity (or other pension) to provide for surviving wives. Most important, women are allowed to keep their own pension in addition to this joint annuity. This means that working women are no longer penalized, as they are in the U.S. and other countries where they must give up their own benefit (to which they have contributed for years) in order to receive the widow's benefit.

Source: **http://www.ncpa.org/pub/st/st264/**

The study went on to suggest that due to "social and economic inequality," women are far more likely to be exploited. It said that women experience more instances of domestic violence than men because of existing social and economic power disparities.

Another study conducted by the National Center for Women and Aging at Brandeis University concurred with NCPA study saying that women who act as caregivers miss out job promotions and pay raises. Consequently, women were less likely to achieve an equal level of financial security than their male counterparts. The report stated that more than two-thirds of caregivers were less likely to receive their "fair" share of retirement or other pension benefits. Researchers interviewed 55 caregivers, who spent more than eight hours a week providing unpaid care to others. It included both those who care for both children and elderly people. Of more than 30 subjects over the age of 45, who had been covered by employer sponsored pensions, caregivers lost an average of more than $639,000 over the course of their earnings lifetime including wages, pension and Social Security benefits. Researchers took 55 caregivers, all women, who spent more than eight hours a week providing unpaid care to others. It included those who care for both children and elderly people. Of more than 30 subjects over the age of 45, the study found that caregivers lost an average of more than $639,000 over the course of their earnings lifetime including wages, pension and Social Security benefits.

> *"Almost seven of ten caregivers reported arriving late or leaving work earlier than normal. Sixty-seven percent reported taking time off during the day to attend to an elderly dependent. Sixty-four percent of respondents said they used sick days or vacation time for caregiving duties. Twenty-two percent said they took a leave of absence, and 20 percent reduced their career from full- to part-time. Sixteen percent quit their jobs, and 13 percent retired early to devote more time to an elderly person.*

> *"Some said caregiving affected their ability to advance at work. Twenty-nine percent said they had passed up a promotion or training assignment, while 25 percent said they had refused a transfer or relocation opportunity because*

of their duties. A smaller percentage said they were not able to acquire new job skills or keep up with important advances in their fields."

Because three-fourths of caretakers are women, the financial consequences of caregiving are more likely to be experienced by women.

Reprinted courtesy of the National Center on Women and Aging, Heller School, Brandeis University, Waltham, MA (02454-9110)

SOCIAL SECURITY AND DEATH

A study conducted by researchers from the University of California San Diego said that Social Security recipients are more likely to die at the beginning of the month than at the end. The year-long study suggested that deaths among minority recipients could be associated to abuse of both alcohol and drugs.

MEDICARE CASE STUDIES

The Sachs Groups, a health care market research firm, conducted a study that revealed a large majority of chronically ill Medicare recipients are satisfied with the health care they receive. Researchers said they were trying to dispel common misconceptions about the inadequacies of Medicare HMO health care system. According to the research group, more than 16,000 chronically ill Medicare recipients in 33 markets participated in the study.

LOSS OF FUNDING STUDY FOR MEDICARE ADVANTAGE RECIPIENTS

According to a study conducted by the Commonwealth Fund, a privately funded charitable organization, moving seniors to private Medicare HMOs is too costly. The study said that taxpayers shell out more than $5.2 billion per year and the numbers will only get worse. On average, the study found the Medicare Advantage plan cost 12.4 percent more than "traditional fee for service" Medicare.

> *In a report about the study issued by United Press International (UPI), proponents of the Advantage plan said increasing the role of the private sector will increase program efficiency. Opponents said "it is this free-market ideology that has led Congress to wastefully subsidize a program that costs more and offers seniors more restricted care.*

WHITE HOUSE STUDY ON MEDICARE

A case study initiated by the White House in 2000 gathered existing health, financial and demographic information of Medicare recipients in attempt to address ongoing problems they believe to be "plaguing" the languishing system. Researchers found that although the poverty level among many elderly Americans has dropped significantly since the program's initiation in 1968, the number of expected beneficiaries is expected to rise to more than 80 million in the next 30 years. In a meeting about the study, White House healthcare advisor Chris Jennings said a lot of work has yet to be done.

According to an article by CNN.com the study states that only 22 percent of U.S. companies offer retiree health insurance with prescription drug coverage, and only one-quarter of Medicare beneficiaries receive such coverage. They went on to state that Medicare has not had the chance to be competitive and efficient in this area and that it does not cover prescription drugs suitably. "Medicare has not been given the tools it needs to be as competitive and efficient as it needs to be in the 21st century. Despite modern medicine's reliance on pharmaceuticals, the program still does not sufficiently cover prescription drugs."

Source: **http://archives.cnn.com/2000/ALLPOLITICS/ stories/02/29/clinton.medicare/index.html**

MORE CASE STUDIES

How do people make decisions?

It is interesting to examine how people make decisions

about personal or business circumstances that affect their lives. This would include anyone, from all walks of life, from your neighbor, your boss, your employee, your doctor, and definitely your Social Security claims examiner. Most of the time, people assume decisions are made in a careful or concise manner when in reality this is far from the truth. According to current research, most decisions come from mental processes people acquire as children. Some research, known as "heuristics," the study of problem solving, has even suggested certain thought processes have been the gift of evolution. They say that as a matter of survival, people developed their abilities to decide matters instinctively. So, why would this matter? The Social Security Administration is a business-oriented environment. Having some idea about how this environment operates may only serve to help you. For example, if you can anticipate how a case examiner may interpret information about you, you can better organize yourself to ensure you get the results you want from them. In effect, if you know how they will decide your fate, the fate of your case may remain secure.

In *Simple Heuristics That Make Us Smart*, researchers from the Max Planck Institute for Human Development conducted an intensive study about how people behave in certain given situations, both business and personal. In most of these situations, researchers found that people when faced with a decision often resort to the "fast and frugal" method. Most of us would probably know this as "multiple guess" type decision-making.

Some researchers speculate this way of making decisions has been "hardwired" into our anatomy because of evolution. To put simply, we have developed a manner of decision-making that has kept us alive and functioning for millions of years. One can imagine that given this information, changing the way we make decisions could prove to be difficult, to say the least.

Three years ago, business author Tom Sant conducted a yearlong study to try and definitively establish whether or not people make decisions based on the fast and frugal method. He conducted an experiment in which he fashioned an accurate, complicated, complex technical proposal to which he then distributed to his clientele. How long did it take for them to make a "keep/discard decision?" In almost every circumstance, Sant said that it took less than six minutes on average for every single one of his clientele to decide against him! One of the key factors in their decisions, Sant said, had to do with "recognition cues." According to Sant's study, "given two objects, one recognizable, the other not, we infer that the recognized object has higher value." To find out more about these cues, Sant conducted another study in which he posed a fictional scenario to people that involved computers, one of which had died. Sant said that when presented with a choice between two computers, people invariably chose the type of computer (and software) that they were familiar with or that in which they recognized, even when the alternative had better or most expensive software, hardware or whatever. To further illustrate his point, Sant proposed an alternate scenario where people were familiar with both types of computers. He found that people's decision-making processes still worked the same. In the alternate situation, people resorted to what Sant called the "single-factor" decision-making process. They no longer held fast to either/or type recognition cues, but this time, they "chose a useful indicator to help them sort among their options." In a sense, people still used recognition cues, but they recognized a tool to help them, rather than place value judgments on unfamiliar objects, as was the case with the scenario involving the unfamiliar computer. Sant's study talked about varieties of single-factor decision making such as "minimalist criteria, using the last" or "taking the best." Basically what this meant was people make decisions: doing the least amount of work possible, doing the same thing they did last time given a similar circumstance, or choosing between several situations that may have generated the most pleasing result. Sant said that people rarely go beyond these three single factors before reaching a decision about anything.

What Does This Have to Do with Me?

Well, first and foremost, this information may impress upon you the important nature of preparation. Your local SSA office is a very business-oriented environment. Have some background knowledge about the rules that govern these arenas. Also, decision makers such as an examiner, an Administrative Law Judge, or Supreme Court Justice are all subject to the same decision making processes as the rest of the people on the planet. Knowing what those processes may be will help. In addition, you have to understand that they will have formulated assumptions about you probably solely based on the papers in your file. As unfair as this might seem, it is often true in many different situations. Try to make sure their assumptions work in your favor. This is possible with proper preparation.

SUMMARY

Chapter 9 covers:

What is a case study?: A case study is a way of determining two things: a problem and a solution to that problem – usually in that order.

Case studies: In a case study conducted by the Center for Retirement Research at Boston College (CRRW), John B. Williamson, a professor of Sociology, stated that people should be careful when examining both successes and failures of privatization between countries whose demographics may vary dramatically.

According to a case study conducted by the Federal Reserve Bank of Cleveland's former senior economic advisor, Jagadeesh Gokhale, privatization will enable everyone, low-income wage earners in particular, to save for their retirement safely. He said investing a portion of Social Security taxes into individualized accounts will generate more "bequeathable" wealth to participants.

According to a case study conducted at the Department of Political Science at Yale University by associate professor Jacob Hacker, the government may have an ulterior motive to privatizing Social Security. He said privatization may simply be a way to hand over money control to "private actors" who are not bound by the same regulations as governmental entities – meaning private businesses are allowed to behave in ways that government is not subject to restrictive regulations.

A case study conducted at the National Academy for Social Insurance (NASI) found that more than half of the nation's Social Security recipients live below the poverty line. According to the data, more than 60 percent of the beneficiaries are elderly widows.

The Center for Budget Policy Priorities (CBPP), a nonpartisan research organization, conducted a national study on how Social Security affects poverty in America. According to the Associated Press, study results released from CBPP suggested that a large portion of both senior and elderly Americans could not sustain themselves financially without benefits. The data suggested that although SSA programs do, in fact, help some in need, a disproportionate amount of citizens are still left unprotected.

A study conducted by the Progressive Policy Institute (PPI) said there will be difficulty ensuring the longevity of Social Security. According to the institute's president, Will Marshall, the problems are mainly due to too much governmental borrowing and partisan politics. He said if something is not done soon, apathy will turn what is currently a manageable problem into "full-blown national crisis."

According to current research, most decisions come from mental processes people acquire as children. Some research, known as "heuristics," the study of problem solving, has even suggested certain thought processes have been the gift of evolution. They say that as a matter of survival, people developed their abilities to decide matters instinctively.

Graduated Pensions: In the 1960s, the United Kingdom initiated legislation to partially privatize its national pension system. "Graduated pensions" were contributions into the British National Insurance program, which mandated that payments were made based on a person's income. Monies were then sectioned into "units" that had their own value worth a predetermined amount.

Stakeholder Pensions: In the United Kingdom, a stakeholder pension works similar to that of a personal pension plan. They are mainly targeted for people who do not have an occupational (or work-related) pension scheme from their place of employment. This enables people who developed a retirement plan for themselves and their families.

"Happiness is like perfume: You can't give it away without getting a little on yourself."

MEDICARE: WHAT IS IT?

HISTORY

Sometime before the 1950s, Harry Truman wrote to Congress asking they try to initiate some form of national health insurance. Although he tried repeatedly, he was not successful in this initiative, as people did not want the country to have publicly managed medical insurance at the time. Medicare was a program later signed into law by President Lyndon Johnson in 1965. No one from the public signed up until 1966. At the signing with his wife and President Johnson, former President Truman was the first person to enroll in the program he had been trying to initiate for more than 20 years. Medicare became a federal insurance program that provided medical care to people over the age of 65. The program then fell into parts. Part I consisted of basic hospital insurance, extended care, home health services, and hospice care for terminally ill patients. Part 2 consisted of a medical insurance program that paid for doctor fees, outpatient, and other services. Some changes to this program came about more than nine years later. In 1973, the program extended services to those who were less than 65 years old and disabled. More than 10 years after that, Congress added coverage for certain illnesses that were considered "catastrophic" and paid for services via a "surtax" or "super tax" on incomes of people who were over the age of 65. By 1993, more than 36 million people were enrolled. By 1997, premiums were about $43 a month.

OPPOSITION TO MEDICARE

In President Johnson's time, and even now, opponents of Medicare vehemently believe the program too expensive, requiring extensive governmental regulation. Opponents of Medicare also said there was undue tax burden put on small business owners. The medical community did not want "socialized medicine" as doctors could only receive an overall salary from the government with an additional stipend, of "fixed amount of money," for each patient. Those who opposed Medicare agreed this form of coverage would reduce the quality of care a person could receive.

SECTION II: PROGRAMS AND SERVICES

Medicare, Now

Medicare is run by the Department Health and Human

Services and its programs have been somewhat extended. Today, Medicare covers more than 41 million people and now has four parts. Part A is for hospital insurance, Part B is for medical insurance, Part C is for health maintenance organization (HMO), and Part D is for prescription coverage. Part D is relatively new and you may add this portion by joining the Medicare Prescription Drug plan.

The Original Medicare Plan, a "fee for service plan," meaning that you are charged only when you get a service, only consists of Part A, but you have the option of adding plans B or D. According to Medicare, the cost is the same each year and for 2008, a deductible will cost you about $135. The balance between what Medicare pays and what you pay goes about 80/20, but you will have to pay a set amount first anyway. Know this plan does not cover all of your health care costs either. Gaps in medical coverage like co-pays or deductibles are not covered. Some experts suggest buying into a supplemental or Medigap policy to cover any additional costs that the main program does not cover. Know that you may only have Medigap if you are on the Original Medicare Plan. The Medicare Advantage Plans cover a little more of the extra costs, but there are some major restrictions on patients who choose HMOs. If you have Medicare Advantage, you will not need Medigap. Also, some people cannot afford to pay more for the other plans (which I will detail later) available under this portion of Medicare.

Basics: With Part A and Part B

If you already collect Social Security when you turn 65 years old, the Medicare Part A cover will be automatic and you will receive your Medicare card in the mail without doing anything on your part. It is free, so make sure your personal information is updated. This does not mean Medicare will pay for all of your costs automatically. Many times people still have to pay deductibles, and other costs incurred when they are admitted to a hospital. Make sure you understand about your benefit periods. This means from the time you enter the hospital and then up to a point where you stop receiving care, about two months after you leave. If you do not receive Social Security, then a good rule of thumb is to sign up about three months before you expect to receive coverage. Part B is optional medical insurance, comes automatically, so if you do not want to receive this portion of service, you will have to contact someone and cancel it. It costs very little so you might want to leave well enough alone. Again, if you are 65 years or older, and have paid your Medicare taxes, you are immediately eligible. There are some circumstances, aside from being over 65 years old, in which you will automatically qualify for Medicare. These circumstances include if you are married to someone who is eligible for Social Security, if you are disabled and have already been collecting Social Security and receiving dialysis, or you have received a kidney transplant. Hospital Insurance (also referred to as the "in-patient" portion), for some, may not be free and you might have to buy into Medicare. This would only happen if you never paid Social Security tax or did not pay into the system long enough. Just like Social Security, a person has to pay into the system to receive benefits later. The rules are that if you have paid a certain number of quarters, usually 40, then you are eligible to receive Medicare for free. If not, or if you have paid less than 40 quarters, you will probably have to pay some additional costs. If you have less than 30 quarters of Medicare employment, your Part A coverage premium as of 2006 will cost $393 per month. This portion of the program consists of coverage that has to do with hospital-related costs. In some circumstances, it may also cover items such as "meals, hospital services and supplies." It may even cover the cost of a semi-private room. Medicare will not pay for a fully private room, unless there is a medical reason. For those who need medical testing, ask your doctor to order "in patient hospital testing." A person needing some kind of extra care may benefit if certain items are a matter of record before he or she leaves the hospital. For example, let us say a patient needs a skilled nursing facility at some point. If the doctor orders the in-patient testing while he or she is there, this will qualify the patient for services provided under Part A of Medicare after he or she leaves. Again, understand that some costs are not fully covered even then. Part B covers outpatient medical and surgical services and supplies. It also covers many diagnostic tests, ambulatory surgery fees, and will even pay for some medical equipment. An example of medical equipment covered under this program would be something like a wheelchair, walker, or hospital bed.

Speech and occupational therapies, outpatient mental health care and physical therapies are also covered under this portion of Part B.

Part C

When Medicare first came about in 1965, the program only had parts A and B. Part C was added in 1997. The intention was to offer people a wider range of services beyond the fee-based programs. Also known as "Medicare+Choice," the program offers several health plans for people to choose from. There is more choice than a person will need, as most Medicare plans consist solely of the HMO portion.

To be eligible to participate in the health plans under Part C, you have to be eligible for Part A and be paying into Part B. Before you start trying to pay for services you cannot receive, try to find out what is available in your area. If you enroll in the Medicare Health Maintenance Organization (HMO), you may only use providers, doctors, and hospital in its network. This means it is going to be difficult for you to keep your own doctor or services you already use. This applies to everyone in every circumstance. You can choose your own primary doctor that will hold sway over other services you many need at some point. To see a specialist, like an endocrinologist, for example, you have to go to your primary doctor first. This gets long and involved during the first go around. The primary doctor then gives you a referral to a specialist, who will invariably refer you to someone else. Know that if you choose this plan, they will not pay for services outside the network. Even if you were to pay additional premiums, the extra money would only allow for partial coverage for what Medicare calls "point of service" (POS). This means sometimes people can keep their own doctor, but they will pay a lot more. Under the Medicare Preferred Provider Plan (PPO), you will have a lot more flexibility than you will with an HMO. It will not cost you as much if you see doctors within their medical network, but it will if you chose to break ranks. In most situations, a person under this plan does not have to go to a primary doctor to be able to see a specialist. Know that the added flexibility will cost considerably more, however. Sometimes, a group of doctors or "medical providers" operate on their own. These are called "Provider-Sponsored Organizations (PSO). Most of them operate (with networks and such) like an HMO with one notable difference. The main difference with this program is the insurer does not dictate what will happen to a patient, as is the case with an HMO. The medical-provider group that consists of doctors and hospitals make the decisions for their patients. There are two more options for those who do not want to be covered under the first three plans. The Private Fee for Service Plan (PFFS) and Medical Savings Account (MSA) require that a person pay a premium along with other costs. Other costs consist of co-pays and deductibles. Currently, the MSAs are no longer available in some areas.

More About Managed Health Care

The term "managed care" was first introduced sometime around the late 1920s and refers to a system of medical care based on prepaid contracts. According to experts, managed health care did not become popular until the 1980s when the skyrocketing cost of health care demanded widespread change. Until then, the traditional style of health care made patients pay when they had a service performed. Go to a doctor, pay then. This is referred to as "fee for service."

Health and Maintenance Organizations or "HMOs" came about with the implementation of the federal Health Maintenance Organization Act of 1973. This law made most U.S. states have an overall standard of health insurance. These federal standards said an HMO "had to provide a comprehensive set of medical services for a prepaid fee with minimal co-payments and could not deny coverage to patients with preexisting illnesses." Organized mainly in two ways, the first type of HMO is typically called a "group practice." This is the type of HMO that has doctors and other health-care related services, along with hospitals, available at its own location. It is not unusual that some of these locations are even owned by the federal government, who in turn has its own group practices, as well. There is current theoretical criticism of this practice as some perceive it is unethical for the government to get personal gain from laws they enact. Smaller forms of government are often not allowed to do this. Some say it is simply a conflict of interest. For example, if I am a city councilman and I own a restaurant, is it acceptable that I have the ability to vote "yes" or "no" on an ordinance that would ultimately generate a ton of money for my business?

Health care providers may be either independent contractors or workers within an HMO. Some of these types of HMO s are referred to as "staff model HMOs." The other, known as "independent practice," provides services via a "contractual relationship," whereby doctors, health care providers, and hospitals are in private practice. Typically, doctors who participate in HMOs get paid a flat rate whether a patient uses their services or not. The fee is paid out to them on a monthly basis. Some HMO critics say this system of managed care may lessen a physician's initiative to do a "good job."

Preferred Provider Organizations or "PPOs," offer more benefits to those who choose their services. This type of managed health care may allow a patient to go "outside" a network. A list containing the names of participating physicians and hospitals is periodically sent to members within the PPO program, but because of recurrent contract negotiations, the list changes quite often. A contract negotiation consists of the PPO trying to get doctor and hospital services at reduced prices. Often times, if a doctor does not meet PPO quality and care standards, they are removed from the physician or hospital list. This does not happen often as the PPO also gives doctors lists of new patients. This means that, in some conditions, a patient has the option to still get coverage and go to any doctor they want. Doctors do however often reserve the right to refuse service to otherwise qualified patients because of personal information they obtain about potential patients provided to them by the PPO. Further, some experts caution people that under a PPO managed care system, the best benefits go to those who stay within the physician network.

Unlike the HMO, the Point of Service Plan (POS) is such that a patient may choose to receive treatment from a physician who is either in or out of a care network. The difference is that a person can choose to pay only when he or she gets treatment, rather than having a doctor get a set fee every month (with an HMO, a doctor gets paid a set amount of money every month whether they see you or not). People who have participated in this program characterize it as a combination of aspects from both HMO and PPO.

Part D

The Plan D program of Medicare has to do with prescription drug coverage. It is not without controversy. According to consumer advocates, this new plan is aimed at maximizing pharmaceutical profits rather than helping seniors get their much-needed prescriptions. Developed as part of a governmental Medicare improvement initiative around 2003, this program came about just two years ago. Beneficiaries now have a lot to choose from and may be a little confused at first. You can add

Plan D, your prescription drug coverage, when you are already part of Medicare plans A or B. This drug plan consists of the Prescription Drug Plan (PDP) and the Medicare Advantage Plan (MA). As the name suggests, the first covers only prescriptions, the second includes both medical services and prescription drugs. This is commonly referred to as "MA-PD."

SUMMARY

Chapter 10 covers:

History of Medicare: The section is a general overview about what the program and where it came from.

Original Medicare Plan: The Original Medicare Plan, a "fee for service plan," means you are charged only when you get a service. It only consists of Part A, but you have the option of adding plans B or D. According to Medicare, the cost is the same each year and for 2008, a deductible will run you about $135.

Medicare Advantage Plan: The Medicare Advantage Plans cover a little more of the extra costs, but there are some major restrictions on patients who choose HMOs. If you have Medicare Advantage, you will not need Medigap.

Plan A: The part of Medicare that has to do with hospital insurance.

Plan B: The part of Medicare that has to do with optional medical insurance.

Plan C: The part of Medicare that is for health maintenance organization (HMO).

HMO: Health and Maintenance Organizations or "HMOs" came about with the implementation of the federal Health Maintenance Organization Act of 1973. Organized mainly in two ways, the first type of HMO is typically called a "group practice." This is the type of HMO that has doctors and other health-care related services, along with hospitals, available at its own location.

PPO: Preferred Provider Organizations or "PPOs" offer more benefits to those who choose their services. This type of managed health care may allow a patient to go "outside" a network.

POS: Unlike the HMO, the Point of Service Plan (POS) is such that a patient may choose to receive treatment from a physician who is either in or out of a care network. The big difference here is that a person can choose to pay only when he or she gets treatment, rather than having a doctor get a set fee every month. People characterize it as a combination of aspects from both HMO and PPO.

Plan D: Plan D program of Medicare has to do with prescription drug coverage.

MORE ABOUT MEDICARE

Chapter 10 covered some basics about what programs are available under Medicare. There is so much information available about programs and services it was difficult to put it all into just one chapter. After interviewing several people, I found there were many things they did not know about Medicare or even how Social Security is related to it. Below is some additional Medicare vocabulary and more information about prescription drug coverage. Also, there is a little background about some relevant information about enrollment, Social Security trust funds, and the future of Medicare.

ALREADY HAVE A PRESCRIPTION PLAN?

Often times, people with retirement benefits or Medicaid have prescription drug coverage plans through alternate sources. If you have COBRA, TRICARE, VA, Federal Employees Health Benefits (FEHB), Program for all Inclusive Care for the Elderly (PACE), End Stage Renal Disease (ESRD), AIDS Drug Assistance Program (ADAP), and State Pharmacy Assistance Program (SPAP) you might not want to alter your current coverage. The status of some of these plans may be subject to change, as well. For example, some states may not have SPAP any longer. Most consumer guides today suggest that beneficiaries contact Medicare before making any new changes to their already existing plans.

What About My Drugs?

There has been some concern as to whether or not the new Plan D will cover certain prescriptions. This is a little confusing, as Medicare has set up their own rules for this. Medicare has a list of drugs they already cover under Plan D. The "tier" (similar to an organization chart) is a way to determine how much your prescriptions will cost. Medicare tells people to incorporate commonly used drugs into their plans. The tier system has types and classes of drugs, as well, so keep that in mind when reviewing it. In most circumstances, generic drugs will be found in the first tier. Also, if you find that the tier does not incorporate one of your drugs, you have option of "getting an exception." This means you will have to go to your doctor and have him or her, as he or she deems appropriate, change you to one of the drugs that is available on the tier system. If you let your doctor know what is going on in advance, the doctor will be able to get you a 30-day grace period in order that you may "safely transition" from one drug to another. If for some reason you simply cannot change drugs, you will have to submit an oral or written statement (along with your doctor's) saying the drug you need is "medically necessary." If you do not do this, there is no way that, if you get denied, that you may go on to the next process – the appeal. Here is what is involved:

1. Ask for a redetermination.

2. If they say "no," ask for the Independent Review Entity (IRE) to review your information.

3. If the IRE says "no," you may have your case review by an Administrative Law Judge.

4. Federal court Judicial Review is the next step if the Administrative Law Judge either says "no," or refuses to hear you case all together. It is unlikely that your case will go this far, but it is nice to know you have the option available.

HOW DO I ENROLL?

Sometimes, companies have enrollment periods that potential beneficiaries must abide by. Initial enrollment into the programs has to be, according to Medicare, "in the seven-month period that begins three months before your 65th birthday and ends three months after your 65th birthday." The periods (called "general enrollment") are from January 1 to March 31 each year. "Special enrollment" periods have to do with whether or not you have some form of existing coverage elsewhere. For example, if you have a plan through your work or your spouse's work, you may opt for this type of enrollment. These enrollment periods are different for many companies, so just keep that in mind when considering what you will do. This is important as some rules mandate that if you do not apply by a certain period, your benefits will most assuredly be delayed which may result in your being charged more money. Sometimes, surcharges can amount to at least ten percent being added to your existing charges. In these circumstances, people waited until well past their birth dates to apply. The time to apply is three or four months before your 65th birthday, but that all depends on what part of the year your birthday falls on. To enroll in Part D, you can get an application and either fax it or mail it back to whatever company interests you the most. A person could either go online and apply or call Medicare at 1-800-633-2273.

WHAT IF I CANNOT AFFORD DRUG COVERAGE?

According to Medicare, there is help if you just cannot afford to pay for any or all of the coverage plans they provide. In some cases, for those who qualify, people do not have to pay premiums under the "extra help" provision. For 2007, if your income was less than $15,315, (or if you are married with a combined income of less than $20,535), and your household resources (assets, for example) are less than $11,710 (or less than

$23,410 if you are married), you may qualify. According to Medicare, however, this number will change in the next year. For some, they may already qualify for the extra help program and not even know it. You may also qualify if you are already receiving SSI benefits, as well.

WHAT A PATIENT NEEDS TO KNOW

After a hospital visit, it is common for people to get a bill in the mail. But there is something that they need to understand. Just because you get a bill in the mail does not mean you are obligated to pay it. Hospital billings departments often do not "talk" to each other. It is conceivable to even receive multiple bills and believe it or not, hospitals often receive double payments, as well. So, if you find yourself in similar circumstances, ask for the bill to be sent to you once more.

The reason why you may not have to pay the full amount for the hospital bill is because of your "deductible." The deductible is just a dollar number that both you and your insurer agree on that you will pay first, before they will pay out compensation on a claim. In Medicare, the deductible is the only part of a hospital bill you need to pay if you were hospitalized for less than 60 days. This is not true in every circumstance because there are times when a person does not even owe a deductible. Remember the "benefit period?" The deductible only needs to be paid when you enter a new benefit period. This is the time from the first day after you leave the hospital until day 59 – in some cases day 61. It is not likely that you would be in the hospital for more than two months, but if so, Medicare will pay some of the bills. In this circumstance, you will be responsible for the "co-payment." About 20 years ago, HMOs introduced a way to lower health care costs. Essentially, hospitals would be paid a flat fee for certain disease types and the general procedures involved in curing those diseases. In addition to the flat fees paid to the hospitals, patients would be directly responsible for fees that had to do with physician visits. Later, these additional fees or "co-payments" were extended to prescriptions as well as some other health related costs. Know that your co-payment will go up the longer you remain in the hospital. After a certain time, Medicare will stop paying the bills all together. This would be at about 150 days. If someone notifies Medicare at about the 90-day mark, a patient would be eligible for "reserves day," but there are only a certain amount of these set aside for patients. You may use them only once while covered under Medicare. Reserve days are typically used almost like buffers between, during or after a patient's benefit period. Medicare will keep track of how many you use, so be sure that you use them wisely.

As stated before, Part B is the optional portion of Medicare that has to do with medical insurance. For this part, the deductible will run about $100, but you may want to verify that when you sign up. For the co-payment, that runs about 20 percent under "approved services and equipment," provided the costs are not mental health related. If they mental health related, your co-payment will run about 50 percent.

Do I Have to Be Sick?

You do not have to be sick to get proper care when Medicare covers you. They have medical services known as "preventative care tests" that can help you before you become ill. You may be covered for some of these tests, provided they fall within the list of accepted tests which include colonoscopy, mammogram screenings, and more. The frequency that Medicare will pay for some of this testing has largely to do with your medical history. They will pay for services every 12 to 48 months, but this depends on what types of testing you need and how often you will need them. There are some services and tests that are not covered under any circumstances. These can include: outpatient prescription drug prescriptions, acupuncture, dental care, cosmetic surgery, hearing aid and hearing related exams, regular foot or eye care, and routine physical exams.

THE FUTURE OF MEDICARE

Experts say that much like Social Security, the future of Medicare is in question. The question that remains is not whether these programs will run out of money. It is just a matter of when the financial well will run dry. In years to come, there will be a disproportionate amount of people who will need Social Security and Medicare benefits. That, in conjunction with the overall rise in cost of living, medical care, and health care, will ultimately put a huge drain on an already burdened system. What causes the rise? Which program will fail first? The trustees for Social Security and Medicare say that in all likelihood, Medicare will run into trouble first. Why? Long-term care under Medicare in 2006 ran at billions of dollars alone.

What Makes Costs Rise?

Medicare is made up of different parts. Parts A and B comprise a percentage of what is known as the "gross domestic product." This refers to all the goods and services made in the U.S. in a year – the cost of making or buying this goes up periodically. Experts predict that in about 12 years, the percentage of the GDP that makes up Part A and B of Medicare is going to more than double. It is also projected to double about every ten years afterward. According to *Medicare for the Clueless*, Medicare currently makes up about 2.3 percent of the GDP. By 2030, this percentage will rise to about 4.6 percent. In 2075, the percent is projected to rise to more than 8.7 percent and so on. They also project that revenues for Social Security and Medicare will decrease and the expenditures for Medicare will far exceed those needed for Social Security.

What Happens Next?

What happens when the trusts run out? Even after the money is spent, remember that Social Security and Medicare payroll taxes will still be coming in. The problem is that this money will only cover a portion of what is needed

– about 75 percent. As years progress, this percentage will decrease proportionally to the GDP. This means there will be less money to pay the bills with.

What Happens to the Other Trusts?

The news in this regard is not much better. Remember those other trust funds? Experts say that the population's income levels will stay the same, while cost rates will rise dramatically. What does this mean? People will have big bills and less money to pay them with. Retirement and Disability funds will be drained in about 30 years. The Hospital Trust Fund will be lost in 20 years. It is projected that payroll taxes will only be able to pay about 30 percent of what it will need. Economists also say that to fix these problems, three things will have to happen: taxes will have to be increased, benefits will decrease, and the government is going to have to cut a chunk of their federal spending. Most agree that it is necessary to change Medicare, but no one is sure how to do that. Proposed changes include: combining Parts A and B of Medicare together, implementing better cost sharing strategies, and reconfiguring how prescription drug coverage should be managed. This proposal is currently a "hot-button" topic as a huge part of the senior population today cannot afford their life-sustaining medication and by 2009, some senior citizens will have to pay more than $200 a week for their drugs. In all likelihood, experts will look at how private insurance companies will weather the economic storm.

SUMMARY

Chapter 11 covers:

Co-payment: HMOs introduce a way to lower health care costs. Essentially, hospitals would be paid a flat fee for certain disease types and the general procedures involved in curing those diseases. In additional to the flat fees paid the hospitals, patients would be directly responsible for fees that had to do with physician visits. Later, these additional fees or "co-payments" were extended to prescriptions as well as some other health related costs.

Already Have A Prescription Plan?: If you have COBRA, TRICARE, VA, Federal Employees Health Benefits (FEHB), Program for all Inclusive Care for the Elderly (PACE), End Stage Renal Disease (ESRD), AIDS Drug Assistance Program (ADAP), and State Pharmacy Assistance Program (SPAP), you might not want to alter your current coverage.

What About My Drugs?: Medicare has a list of drugs they already cover under Plan D. The "tier" (similar to an organization chart) is a way to determine how much your prescriptions will cost. Medicare tells people to incorporate commonly used drugs into their plans. The tier system also has types and classes of drugs, so keep that in mind when reviewing it. In most circumstances, generic drugs will be found in the first tier. Also, if you find that the tier does not incorporate one of your drugs, you have option of "getting an exception." This means you will have to go to your doctor and have him or her, as he or she deems appropriate, change you to one of the drugs that is available on the tier system.

Enrollment: Companies have enrollment periods potential beneficiaries must abide by. Initial enrollment into the programs has to be, according to Medicare, "in the seven-month period that begins three months before your 65th birthday and ends three months after your 65th birthday." The periods (called "general enrollment") are from January 1 to March 31 each year. "Special enrollment" periods have to do with whether or not you have some form of existing coverage elsewhere.

Deductible: The deductible is a dollar number that both you and your insurer agree on that you will pay first, before they will pay out compensation on a claim.

Extra Help Provisions: According to Medicare, there is help if you cannot afford to pay for any or all of the coverage plans they provide. In some cases, for those who qualify, people do not have to pay premiums under the "extra help" provision.

Patient Needs to Know: It is common that after a hospital visit, people get a bill in the mail. But there is something that they need to understand. Just because you get a bill in the mail does not mean you are obligated to pay it. Hospital billing departments often do not "talk" to each other. It is conceivable to even receive multiple bills and believe it or not, hospitals often receive double payments, as well.

The Future of Medicare: Experts say that much like Social Security, the future of Medicare is in question. The question that remains is not whether these programs will run out of money. It is just a matter of when the financial well will run dry.

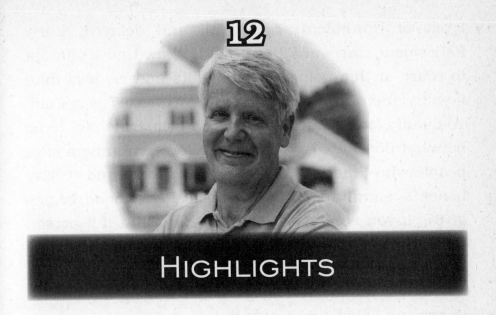

HIGHLIGHTS

The history of social interest in western society has been a long and tumultuous one. As societies have changed over the years, social aid initiatives have changed with them. The development of 1800 B.C. estate laws, 16th-century English poor laws, the initiation of early America's fraternal orders, the Townsend Club, and the Social Security Act were all rooted in this premise. Since the Social Security Act of 1935, there have been many subsequent laws that indeed did recognize the need for change. Empathy is one ideal, however, that should remain consistent in a vast wasteland of social complexity that may invariably come.

SOCIAL SECURITY RETIREMENT

The main thing to remember is there are three different

types of retirement: early, full and delayed. Early Retirement starts at 62 years old. Know that if you opt to retire at this point, your benefits may be less than if you waited until your were 65, or even 67 years old. To qualify for Full Retirement, you primarily have to be between 65 and 67 years old. In some circumstances, people who take full retirement may work and receive benefits simultaneously. Delayed Retirement begins at 67, if you so choose. According to SSA, if a person takes this type of retirement, he or she may receive a larger amount of benefits than either Early or Full. The amount of money you may receive during any one of the above listed types of retirement depends on your earnings record. SSA calculates your wage earnings over a course of time – usually, the 35 years of your life in which you made the most money. Everyone who has worked, whether they were self-employed or not, can receive Social Security retirement, provided they have just worked "long enough." If you have worked consistently for more than 20 years, you and your family will probably qualify for money from any one of the retirement programs.

DISABILITY BENEFITS

You can qualify as disabled if you are unable to "engage in any substantial gainful activity by reason of any medically determinable physical or mental impairment which can be expected to result in death or has lasted or can be expected to last for a continuous period of not less than 12 months." This disability needs to be "medically determinable." That means if a doctor says (remember there are different types of doctors) you are disabled (usually meaning that you have been incapacitated and will not recover for more than three months), SSA will probably agree. They have a five-step process in evaluating anyone who applies for benefits, and this includes children. SSA will probably be a little more compassionate with a child's disability, but SSA will still require a step by step analysis of any application. One primary issue regarding children's cases is they must have a severe functional limitation, according to SSA.

The two types of disability benefits are Social Security Disability Insurance (SSDI) and Supplemental Security Income (SSI). SSDI is for adults who are impaired because of a medical condition. SSI is for generally for people who have a lower income than those who qualify for SSDI. People who qualify for this program usually have limited money and resources to assist themselves. SSA will enable you to receive benefits during your application process by way of presumptive disability. This means you can get money because SSA will presume that you will qualify for other types of benefits once your application has been approved and completed. If you do not qualify for presumptive disability, you may want to try for conditional benefits. However, under this program, you may have to pay back in full any monies you receive.

Disability for children works almost the same way as it does for adults. Examiners will mainly be concerned with whether or not your child meets initial criteria. According to SSA guidelines, a child will have to be severely functionally impaired or limited. This will mainly have to do with if a child is developmentally, whether physically or mentally, inhibited. Additionally, a child cannot earn above a certain amount of money. Current SSA guidelines dictate the dollar amount cannot exceed $900 a month. Know there are some circumstances this rule may not apply.

OTHER SOCIAL SECURITY BENEFIT PROGRAMS

Dependent benefits are for people who rely on you financially. Both biological children and stepchildren qualify under this condition. Primarily, they qualify if they are unmarried, under 18 years old, or if they are a student between the ages of 18 and 19 (22 years old, if disabled). According to the SSA, about three months before your qualifying child turns 18, you will receive notification that benefits will stop. If your child is still in high school, but over 18-years old, there are some conditions when benefits are kept in place until the child graduates from high school. The SSA will require some verification of this, however. Some kind of confirmation from a reliable school official will suffice as proper confirmation. Survivor benefits protect loved ones financially in the event of an unexpected death. Spouses and children generally qualify for assistance under this program. SSA will require a death certificate, a marriage certificate, and Social Security numbers for all family members; the deceased worker's tax return; and bank account information, if applicable.

EMPLOYERS, EMPLOYEES, AND SELF-EMPLOYED

Everyone who works is going to have to do paper work at some point whether it is for taxes or eventually even Social Security. Primarily, employees need to complete a W-4 and submit it to their employer. An employer is required to give every new employee this piece of paper when he or she is first hired. It is technically referred to as an "Employee Withholding Allowance Certificate." It is a way for the government to know something about your living and financial situation. They may refer to this as "exemption status." It is also a way for them to categorize you. If your circumstances change, you may consider refilling every year whether you change jobs or not. It might help you in the end. Depending on what exemptions you claim, this will determine how you are categorized and will also determine what deductions you will eventually be able to see on your paychecks. As I stated earlier, this is what is commonly referred to as the "Federal Contributions Insurance Act" or "FICA." Medicare, which I will detail later, is also a secondary amount deducted.

Employers have a little more work to do in this respect, however. Overall, they need to keep track of who works for them and how much money they make. They will also need to give proof and submit their information to the government periodically. Employers are usually assigned a Tax ID number and this is how the government will generally identify them. They are responsible for W-2s, as well.

Self-employed people have to cover both the employee and the employer aspects of tax paperwork. Social Security will treat self-employed people a little differently, as well. The percentages of taxes are a bit higher, but self-employed people get a tax break later on.

State and Local Employees have a wider range of opportunity to receive benefits during the course of their careers. They also may have better access to Social Security benefits, if they so choose, as they have access to pensions, benefits, and other income sources most people do not. The Windfall Elimination Provision is one vehicle by which the government tried to level the "playing field," a bit.

UNEMPLOYMENT COMPENSATION

This type of benefit is financial protection afforded to people who have lost their jobs. The program is paid for by business payrolls and recipients may only receive benefits for a limited time. The duration can range from anywhere between 26 to 65 weeks. People who receive unemployment generally get a portion of what they would have received had they still been able to work. Each state has its own requirement as to exactly what amount this may entail. To qualify for unemployment a person has to primarily have worked for a covered employer. A person has to have worked for a period of time before they can expect to get benefits. The money is usually contingent on how much income a person has made before they became unemployed. To continue to receive unemployment, a person has to be looking for a job as soon as he or she is able. Your benefits may be discontinued if you refuse employment. Again, each state has its own rules about terms. If at any point, you are denied or have your benefits discontinued, they are processes in place that may enable you to extend your benefits. Requests for Reconsideration and Administrative Appeals are just two examples.

PROGRAMS OUTSIDE OF SOCIAL SECURITY

In some circumstances people do not qualify for Social Security and many assistance programs exist just for this reason. If you need financial help while you are applying for Social Security, for example, alternative programs out there often have similar benefits to that of Social Security. For whatever reason you may need assistance, know there are many federal, state, and other local agencies that can help. Many social organizations, churches, schools, doctors offices have phone lists, addresses and e-mails or other information that will help you find the assistance you need You can probably find any number of these programs in your area. In some cities, you may be able to dial "211" on any phone. This is a valuable emergency resource information tool. Here is a quick list of some others:

- Temporary Assistance for Needy Families (TANF) – **http://www.acf.hhs.gov/programs/ofa**

- Food Stamp Program & EBT – 1-888-356-3281 or **http://www.fns.usda.gov/fsp/ebt**

- Women, Infants and Children (WIC) – **http://www.fns.usda.gov/wic**

- Partnership for Prescription Assistance Program – **www.pparx.org**

- Assistance for Infants and Toddlers with Disabilities – **http://www.nectac.org/partc/partc.asp**

- Low-Income Home Energy Assistance – **http://www.acf.hhs.gov/programs/liheap**

- Emergency Food Assistance Program – **http://www.fns.usda.gov/fdd/programs/tefap**

- RxAssist – **www.rxassist.org**

- Special Milk Program – **http://www.fns.usda.gov/cnd/milk**

- Independent Services for Older and Blind Individuals – **http://www.ed.gov/programs/rsailob/index.**html

- Freedom From Hunger – **http://www.freedomfromhunger.org**

- The Salvation Army – **http://www. salvationarmyusa.org/usn/www_usn.nsf**

SYSTEM IN DANGER

Believe it or not, the baby boomers are not solely responsible for the problems with Social Security. It appears that every problem needs a "scapegoat." The system is structured in such a way as to not guarantee money to people who have paid into it for years. That is a problem. The problem is there is currently little accountability for people in the government who perpetually mismanage your money. The Supreme Court has said that even if a person spends a lifetime paying their taxes, the government does not have to "ante-up" when you may need your money the most. For example, let us say a private "citizen" (should we call him "Uncle Sam?") accepted money from people, who in all likelihood expected at least some money back eventually. Years and years go by and this "citizen" tells his investors (for lack of a better term) that everything is "all right," and to just keep working and paying. Now someone needs his or her money for his or her retirement, disability, or unexpected death, for example. The "citizen" then tells this person that he never "guaranteed" to pay any money back. The person who paid into the "citizen security" during the course of his or her work lifetime can no longer sustain him or herself. In reality, the "citizen" has spent the worker's money elsewhere without care or even permission. Now the worker, for whatever reason, is unable to work. As he or she is no longer able to contribute to the money train, he or she is left without aid or consideration.

Yes, the number of old people will rise, but there are other variables that will facilitate the demise of Social Security – the main of which is apathy. Social Security works as a "pay as you go" program. As stated earlier, the program is funded by money people pay into right now. Later, the money paid into it will come from other future workers, like your sons, daughters, or whomever. There are arguments on both sides of the proverbial governmental table about whether or not Social Security is even in any danger or not. One side says the money will run out and to "be afraid, be very afraid." Another tells us the scare tactic is simply a sham to divert attention. It is hard to tell what to believe.

HELP, I HAVE BEEN DENIED!

There are various reasons why people are denied Social Security or Medicare benefits. Many experts report that people are often denied simply due to lack of appropriate paperwork or other corresponding information. For example, something as simple as not turning in your paperwork on time (or before said date) could prove to be disastrous. To avoid mistakes, make sure to call your case worker or examiner as often as you can. They may not appreciate your diligence, but at least you will receive the benefits you need. If your application for benefits is delayed, terminated or outright denied, know there are measures that you can take to ensure that you have not been rejected unduly. Filing a request for reconsideration is the first action you will need to take in the event there is ever a problem. Subsequent appeals or other actions may be taken only after this initial process is completed.

INSIGHTS

Professional perspective is always a good thing whether you may agree with it or not. Some experts have a wealth of information to provide, the trick is to know where to look. Case studies are valuable, not so much in that they provide scientifically provable information, but they may assist people in finding solutions to problems that they have not thought about before. If you did it right, that is. Social scientists, statisticians, and even some project management personnel often mistakenly formulate a study result before they delineate a problem to begin with. In this circumstance, the "puzzle" gets adjusted a little in reverse. Know that results from case studies conducted backwards may appear polluted. This will dramatically inhibit the ability to find clear-cut solutions. Privatization is a concept whereby a transfer of something to private ownership takes place. Proponents and opponents constantly battle each other about whether or not this concept is applicable to Social Security. Other countries have tried it and have had some moderate success. The problem with this is cross culturally, some concepts may not work the way we want them to. So quantifying another's successes or failures in this respect may not be the way to go. It may warrant further consideration. Advocates of privatization say it is an effective money-making tool. Opponents say that the positive affects of privatization will only be felt by a privileged few and that people outside majority economic margins (or culture margins, if you prefer), will be made to suffer immeasurably. In this respect, majority should not rule.

People make decisions in various ways and researchers study decision making processes so they may learn how to better understand the way a human mind works. If one can generally understand how people may come to think and feel the things that they do, they may better communicate wants and desires to each other.

MEDICARE

Although Medicare did not come about until the 1960s, it was a subject of much discussion long before that. Signed into law by President Lyndon Johnson in 1966, Medicare became a federal insurance program that provided medical care to people over the age of 65. The term "managed care" was first introduced sometime around the late 1920s and refers to a system of medical care based on prepaid contracts. According to experts, managed health care did not become popular until the 1980s when the skyrocketing cost of health care demanded widespread change. Until then, the traditional style of health care made patients pay when they had a service performed. Go to a doctor, and pay then. This is referred to as "fee for service."

Health and Maintenance Organizations or "HMOs" came about with the implementation of the federal Health Maintenance Organization Act of 1973. These laws made most U.S. states have an overall standard of health insurance. These federal standards said an HMO "had to provide a comprehensive set of medical services for a prepaid fee with minimal co-payments and could not deny coverage to patients with preexisting illnesses." Organized mainly in two ways, the first type of HMO is typically called a "group practice." This is the type of HMO that has doctors and other health-care related services, along with hospitals, available at its own location. It is not unusual that some of these locations are even owned by the federal government, who in turn has its own group practices, as well. Preferred Provider Organizations or "PPOs" offer more benefits to those who choose their services. This type of managed health care may allow a patient to go "outside" a network.

The Medicare program generally falls into parts: Part A, B, C, and now D. The original Medicare Plan, a "fee for service plan," meaning that you are charged only when you get a service, only consists of Part A, but you have the option of adding plans B or D. Medicare Advantage programs give people the option of going to private insurance companies for their coverage. If you enroll in the Medicare Health Maintenance Organization (HMO), you may only use providers, doctors, and hospital in its network. Part D is a more recent addition to Medicare and has to do with prescriptions. There are various choices, but this program mainly consists of the Prescription Drug Plan (PDP) and the Medicare Advantage Plan (MA). Point of Service Plan (POS) is such that a patient may choose to receive treatment from a physician who is either in or out of a care network.

FUTURE OF MEDICARE

Experts say that much like Social Security, the future of Medicare is in question. The question that remains is not whether these programs will run out of money. It is just a matter of when the financial well will run dry. In years to come, there will be a disproportionate amount of people who will need Social Security and Medicare benefits. That, in conjunction with the overall rise cost of living, medical care, and health care, will ultimately put a huge drain on an already burdened system. Costs rise because Medicare is made of parts of the GDP (this has to do with goods and services made in the United States and this cost rises as the cost of making or buying items rises, too). The costs of Medicare Part A and B, according to many experts, will more than double in about 12 years. It may also double about every ten years after that. Even after the money is spent, Social Security and Medicare payroll taxes will still be coming in. The problem is this money will only cover a portion of what is needed – about 75 percent. As years progress, this percentage will decrease proportionally to the GDP. This means there will be less money for people to pay their bills with.

TRUST FUNDS

Experts say that the population's income levels will stay the same for many years, while cost rates will rise dramatically. Retirement and Disability funds will be drained in about 30 years. The Hospital Trust Fund will be lost in 20 years. It is projected that payroll taxes will only be able to pay about 30 percent of what it will need. Economists also say that to fix these problems, three things will have to happen: taxes will have to be increased, benefits will decrease, and the government is going to have to cut a chunk of their federal spending. Most agree that it is necessary to change Medicare, but no one is sure how to do that. Proposed changes include: combining Parts A and B of Medicare together, implementing better cost sharing strategies, and reconfiguring how prescription drug coverage should be managed.

"I've learned that everyone wants to live on top of the mountain, but all the happiness and growth occurs while you're climbing it."

CONCLUSION

When asked about coping with difficulty, Greek philosopher Plato once said, "There's a victory and defeat – the first and best of victories, the lowest and worst of defeats – which each man gains or sustains at the hands not of another, but of himself." Put more simply, whenever a person is met with hardship, there are generally two variables to their circumstance – they can win or they can lose. According to Plato, there are degrees of winning and losing, as well. A person does not move forward or back in a moment of difficulty because of what someone else does or does not "do" to them. They are held responsible – alone and accountable for their successes or failures in life.

So there it is. Everything you need to know, right? Well, probably not everything. There is so much information about Social Security and Medicare one would need at least several volumes in order to cover everything.

Remember when considering Social Security, whether you are applying for retirement, disability, survivor, unemployment, or other kinds of benefits, know what you want to have happen for either you or your family. If possible, minimize frustration from the beginning by having a plan.

Politicians, advocacy experts, economists, and the lot, all have something to say lately about Social Security and Medicare. Throughout their political maneuvering, they seem to forget the programs are there for you. As stated in the beginning of this book, it is unlikely that any of them will have to worry at length about their financial circumstances. Know that it is easy to become lost in all the regulatory complexity, so empower yourself with information. Education is the key tool with which you will ensure, at least partially, economic security for both you and your loved ones. Given this, it is less likely that a disgruntled case manager or an apathetic claims or disability examiner (not to suggest that all are bad), will be able to take advantage of you. In this, you have to at least appear as if you know what it is you are talking about. Be sure your knowledge applies directly to your circumstances, too. Do not let a case worker give you the proverbial "we have to treat everyone the same." Everyone is not the same and different circumstances call for flexibility, so demand it. Know that if you need help, there are a lot of genuinely good people and resources available to you. Find a person who you trust if you have any questions or concerns along the way. If all else fails, be sure you have them explain it to you simply.

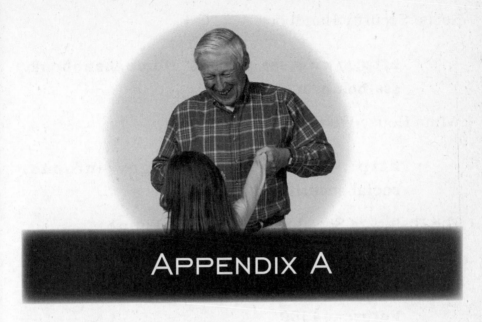

APPENDIX A

INTERNET RESOURCES

Social Security Around the World

- **http://www.socialsecurity.gov/foreign/index.html**

Social Security Online History Page

- **http://www.ssa.gov/history/history.html**

Genealogy Today: Social Security History

- **http://www.genealogytoday.com/guide/help/ssa.html**

Library of Congress

- **http://www.loc.gov/index.html**

Social Security Handbook

- **http://www.ssa.gov/OP_Home/handbook/ ssa-hbk.htm**

White House Web site

- **http://www.whitehouse.gov/infocus/ social-security**

The History of Social Security and Its Future

- **http://www.socyberty.com/Government/ The-History-of-Social-Security-and-its- Future-.44389**

Basic Projects: The History of Social Security in the U.S.

- **http://www.basicsproject.org/social_ security_reform/history_of_social_security_ in_the_us.htm**

Retirement and Auxiliary Benefits

- **http://www.ssa.gov/retirement.html**
- **http://www.socialsecurity.gov/retire2/near. htm**
- **http://www.aarp.org/money/social_security**
- **http://www.nolo.com/resource.cfm/catID/ A74E92D1-EE6C-420C-B64B7FCB6A2953 A8/213/233**

Disability Benefits

- http://www.ultimatedisabilityguide.com
- http://www.ssa.gov/disability
- http://www.4socialsecuritydisability.net
- http://www.nosscr.org/faqind.html
- http://www.socialsecurity.gov/wounded warriors
- http://www.disabilityinfo.gov/digov-public/ public/DisplayPage.do?parentFolderId=500

Dependent and Survivor Benefits

- http://www.ssa.gov/OP_Home/ssact/ title02/0226A.html
- http://www.ssa.gov/pubs/10084.html
- http://www.ssa.gov/pubs/10018.html
- http://money.cnn.com/2004/04/06/pf/ expert/ask_expert/index.htm
- http://www.irs.gov/faqs/faq6.html

Lump Sum Payments

- http://en.allexperts.com/q/Disability-Law-917/ Lump-sum-payment-receiving.htm
- http://en.allexperts.com/q/Disability-Law-917/ disabilty-lump-sum-payment.htm

- http://www.ssdanswers.com/2007/03/07/
tax-treatment-of-ssdi-benefits-and-lump-
sum-payments

- http://community.federalsoup.com/4/Open
Topic?a=tpc&s=4944011921&f=6984011031
&m=3961026851

- http://www.rrb.gov/forms/PandS/rb21/
rb21part2.asp

Special Coverage Provisions

- http://public.findlaw.com/bookshelf-ssa-
handbook/handbook.09/handbook-toc09.
html

- http://www.ssa.gov/OP_Home/ssact/
title02/0226A.htm

Employer/Employee Relationship

- http://www.ssa.gov/OP_Home/handbook/
handbook.08/handbook-toc08.html

- http://www.ssa.gov/OP_Home/handbook/
handbook.08/handbook-0800.html

- http://www.ssa.gov/OP_Home/handbook/
handbook.08/handbook-0801.html

- http://www.ssa.gov/OP_Home/handbook/
handbook.08/handbook-0802.html

- http://www.ssa.gov/OP_Home/handbook/
handbook.08/handbook-0830.html

Employer/Employee Filing

- http://www.socialsecurity.gov/employer/ssnv.htm

- http://www.socialsecurity.gov/employer/critical.htm

Self Employed Information

- http://www.socialsecurity.gov/pubs/10022.html

State and Local Employees

- http://www.ssa.gov/slge

Other Helpful Web Sites

- http://www.aoa.gov

- http://www.cms.hhs.gov/default.asp?

- http://www.usa.gov

- http://www.ncd.gov

- http://www.whitehouse.gov

- http://www.ahcpr.gov

- http://www.census.gov

- http://www.gsa.gov/Portal/gsa/ep/home.do?tabId=0

- http://www.pbgc.gov

- http://www.mymoney.gov

- http://thomas.loc.gov

- http://www.medicare.gov

- http://www.cms.hhs.gov/home/medicaid.asp?

- http://www.senate.gov

- http://www.va.gov

- http://www.wclp.org

APPENDIX B

Social Security Economists and Policy Experts

1025 Connecticut Ave. NW
Suite 205
Washington, DC 20036
TEL: 202-955-5665
Fax: 202-955-5606
www.ourfuture.org

Roger Hickey
Co-Director
Campaign for America's
Future
Washington, DC
Phone: 202-955-5665
http://www.ourfuture.org

Adam Luna
Director, Social Security

Information Project
Institute for America's Future
Washington, DC
Phone: 202-955-5665
http://www.ourfuture.org

Henry Aaron, PhD
Chair, Advisory Council on
Social Security, 1979
Senior Fellow, Economic
Studies
The Brookings Institution
Washington, DC
Phone: 202-797-6000
http://www.brookings.edu

Nancy Altman
Founding Board Member
National Academy of Social
Insurance

Chairman of the Board of
Directors
Pension Rights Center
Washington, DC
Phone: 301-229-2651
**http://www.pensionrights.
org**

Greg Anrig
Vice President, Programs
The Century Foundation
New York, NY
Phone: 212-452-7724
http://www.tcf.org

Kenneth Apfel
Commissioner, Social Security
Administration, 1997-2001
Sid Richardson Chair in
Public Affairs, Lyndon B.
Johnson School of Public
Affairs
University of Texas at Austin
Austin, Texas
Phone: 512-471-6267
**http://www.utexas.edu/lbj/
faculty/apfel**

Dean Baker, PhD
Co-Director
Center for Economic and
Policy Research
Washington, DC
Phone: 202-293-5380
http://www.cepr.net

Edward Berkowitz, PhD
Professor of History
George Washington University
Washington, DC
Phone: 202-994-8174
http://columbian.gwu.edu

Kim Gandy
President of the National
Organization for Women
Washington, DC
Phone: 202-628-8669
http://www.now.org

Theresa Ghilarducci, PhD
Advisory Board Member,
Pension Benefit Guaranty
Corporation, 1995-2002
Associate Professor of
Economics
University of Notre Dame
Notre Dame, IN
Phone: 574-631-7581
http://www.nd.edu/~krocinst

Fernando Torres Gil, PhD
Associate Dean, Academic
Affairs
Director, Center for Policy
Research on Aging
University of California, Los
Angeles
Los Angeles, CA
Phone: 310-206-1994
http://www.sppsr.ucla.edu

Austan Goolsbee, PhD
Professor of Economics
University of Chicago School
of Business
Chicago, IL
Phone: 773-702-5869
**http://gsbwww.uchicago.
edu/fac/austan.goolsbee/
website**

Robert Greenstein
Founder and Executive
Director
Center on Budget and Policy
Priorities
Washington, DC
Phone: 202-408-1080
http://www.cbpp.org

Heidi Hartmann, PhD
President and CEO
Institute for Women.s Policy
Research
Washington, DC
Phone: 202-785-5100
http://www.iwpr.org

Hon. Barbara Kennelly
President and CEO
National Committee to
Preserve Social Security and
Medicare
Washington, DC
Phone: 800-966-1935
http://www.ncpssm.org

Eric Kingson, PhD
Founding Board Member
National Academy of Social
Insurance
Professor of Social Work and
Public Administration
School of Social Work, College
of Human Services and Health
Professions
Syracuse University
Syracuse, NY
Phone: 315-443-1838
Email: erkingso@syr.edu

George Kourpias
Advisory Council on Social
Security, 1994-1996
President
Alliance for Retired Americans
Washington, DC
Phone: 202-974-8222
**http://www.
retiredamericans.org**

Paul Krugman, PhD
Professor of Economics and
International Affairs, Woodrow
Wilson School of Public and
International Affairs
Princeton University
Princeton, NJ
Phone: 609-258-4570
**http://www.wws.princeton.
edu/~pkrugman**

Richard C. Leone
President
Century Foundation
New York, NY
Phone: 212-535-4441
http://www.tcf.org

Charles Leven
Vice President - Board
Governance/Board Chair/
AARP
Washington, DC
Phone: 202-434-2560
http://www.aarp.org

Theodore R. Marmor, PhD
Professor of Public Policy and
Political Science
Yale University
New Haven, CT
Phone: 203-432-3238
http://mba.yale.edu

Max Sawicky, PhD
Economist
Economic Policy Institute
Washington, DC
Phone: 202-331-5531
http://www.epinet.org

James H. Schulz, PhD
Professor Emeritus,
Economics, Florence Heller
School
Brandeis University
Waltham, MA

Phone: 603-664-5361
http://www.brandeis.edu

Robert Y. Shapiro, PhD
Professor of Political Science,
School of International and
Public Affairs
Columbia University
New York, NY
Phone: 212-854-3944
http://www.sipa.columbia.edu

Gerald Shea
Member, Social Security
Advisory Board
Advisory Council on Social
Security, 1994-1996
Assistant to the President for
Government Affairs
AFL-CIO
Washington, DC
Phone: 202-637-5000
http://www.aflcio.org

Hilary O. Shelton
Director, Washington Bureau
NAACP
Washington, DC
Phone: 202-463-2940
http://www.naacp.org

Max Skidmore, PhD
Curators. Professor of Political
Science
University of Missouri at

Kansas City
Kansas City, MO
Phone: 816-235-2535
**http://www.umkc.edu/
iphd/iphd.html**

Gene Sperling
Senior Fellow
Center for American Progress
Washington, DC
Phone: 202-682-1611
**http://www.
americanprogress.org**

William Spriggs, PhD
Senior Fellow
Economic Policy Institute
Washington, DC
Phone: 202-775-8810
http://www.epinet.org

Bernard Wasow, PhD
Senior Fellow
The Century Foundation
Washington, DC
Phone: 202-745-5491
http://www.tcf.org

Marilyn Watkins, PhD
Policy Director
Economic Opportunity
Institute
Seattle, WA
Phone: 206-529-6370
http://www.eoionline.org

Mark Weisbrot
Co-Director
Center for Economic and
Policy Research
Washington, DC
Phone: 202-293-5380
http://www.cepr.net

Christian Weller, PhD
Senior Economist
Center for American Progress
Washington, DC
Phone: 202-682-1611
**http://www.
americanprogress.org**

Joseph White, PhD
Director, Center for Policy
Studies
Case Western Reserve
University
Cleveland, OH
Phone: 216-368-2426
http://www.case.edu

Edward Wolff, PhD
Senior Scholar, Levy Institute
of Economics at Bard College
Professor of Economics
New York University
New York, NY
Phone: 212-998-8917
**http://www.econ.nyu.edu/
user/wolffe**

Laurie Young
Executive Director
OWL - The Voice of Midlife
and Older Women
Washington, DC
Phone: 202-783-6686
http://www.owl-national.org

Social Security Administration Regional Directors

(Boston)
Kurt Czarnowski
Room 1900, JFK Building
Government Center
Boston, MA 02203
Phone: 617-565-2881
Fax: 617-565-2143
Email: bos.rcd@ssa.gov

(Chicago)
Carmen M. Moreno
600 West Madison Street
10th Floor
Chicago, IL 60661
Phone: 312-575-4050
Fax: 312-575-4051
Email: chi.rpa@ssa.gov

(Denver)
Jan Foushee
Federal Office Building, Room 1052

1961 Stout Street
Denver, CO 80294-3538
Phone: 303-844-1888
Fax: 303-844-3674
Email: den.rcd@ssa.gov

(Atlanta)
Nathan L. Holmes
Atlanta Federal Center
61 Forsyth Street, S.W., Ste 23T29
Atlanta, GA 30303
Phone: 404-562-5500
Fax: 404-562-5506
Email: atl.orc.rpa@ssa.gov

(New York)
John Shallman
Room 40-102
26 Federal Plaza
New York, NY 10278
Phone: 212-264-2500
Fax: 212-264-1444
Email: ny.rpa@ssa.gov

(Dallas)
Wes Davis
SSA/Public Affairs
1301 Young Street, Room 1052
Dallas, TX 75202-5433
Phone: 214-767-3407
Fax: 214-767-8986
Email: da.rpa@ssa.gov

(San Francisco)
Leslie Walker
P.O. Box 4201
1221 Nevin Avenue, 6W
Richmond, CA 94804
Phone: 510-970-8430
Fax: 510-970-8218
Email: leslie.s.walker@ssa.gov
or sf.rpa@ssa.gov

(Philadelphia)
Terri Lewis
7th Floor
300 Spring Garden St.
Philadelphia, PA 19123
Phone: 215-597-3747
Fax: 215-597-1415
Email: phi.rpa@ssa.gov

(Kansas City)
John Garlinger
Bolling Federal Building,
Room 436
601 East 12th Street
Kansas City, MO 64106
Phone: 816-936-5740
Fax: 816-936-5727
Email: kc.rpao@ssa.gov

(Seattle)
Joy Chang
Suite 2900, M/S 301
701 Fifth Avenue
Seattle, WA 98104-7075
Phone: 206-615-2660

Fax: 206-615-2097
Email: sea.orc.rpa@ssa.gov

Other Resources:

60 Plus Association
E-Mail: info@60plus.org
1600 Wilson Blvd., Suite 960
Arlington, VA 22209
Phone: 703-807-2070
Fax: 703-807-2073
http://www.60plus.org

Alliance for Retired Americans
E-Mail: webform
815 16th St. NW, Fourth Floor
Washington, DC 20006
Phone: 202-637-5399
**http://www.
retiredamericans.org**

American Association for
Retired Persons
E-Mail: member@aarp.org
601 E St. NW
Washington, DC 20049
Phone: 202-434-2277,
800-424-3410
Fax: 202-434-6484
http://www.aarp.org

American Geriatrics Society
E-Mail: info@
americangeriatrics.org
Empire State Building

350 5th Ave., Suite 801
New York, NY 10118
Phone: 212-308-1414
Fax: 212-832-8646
**http://www.
americangeriatrics.org**

National Council on the Aging
E-Mail: info@ncoa.org
300 D St. SW, Suite 801
Washington, DC 20024
Phone: 202-479-1200
Fax: 202-479-0735
TDD: 202-479-6674

http://www.ncoa.org

National Indian Council on
Aging
E-Mail: dave@nicoa.org
10501 Montgomery Blvd. NE,
Suite 210
Albuquerque, NM 87111-3846
http://www.nicoa.org

Concord Coalition
E-Mail: concordcoalition@
concordcoalition.org
1011 Arlington Blvd., Suite
300
Arlington, VA 22209
Phone: 703-894-6222
Fax: 703-894-6231
**http://www.
concordcoalition.org**

Generations United
E-Mail: gu@gu.org
1333 H St. NW, Suite 500W
Washington, DC 20005
Phone: 202-289-3979
Fax: 202-289-3952
http://www.gu.org

National Committee to
Preserve Social Security and
Medicare
E-Mail: general@ncpssm.org
10 G St. NE, Suite 600
Washington, DC 20002-4215
Phone: 202-216-0420,
800-966-1935
Fax: 202-216-0451
http://www.ncpssm.org

Third Millennium
E-Mail: thirdmil@juno.com
330 W 38th St., Suite 1705
New York, NY 10018
Phone: 212-760-4240
http://www.thirdmil.org

National League of Cities
E-Mail: weekly@nlc.org
1301 Pennsylvania Ave. NW,
Suite 550
Washington, DC 20004
Phone: 202-626-3000
Fax: 202-626-3043
http://www.nlc.org

NAACP Legal Defense and
Education Fund
99 Hudson St.
New York, NY 10013
Phone: 212-965-2200
Fax: 212-226-7592
http://www.naacpldf.org

National Association for the
Advancement of Colored
People (NAACP)
4805 Mt. Hope Dr.
Baltimore, MD 21215
Phone: 877-NAACP-98,
410-521-4939
Fax: 410-486-9257
http://www.naacp.org

National Urban League
E-Mail: info@nul.org
120 Wall St.
New York, NY 10005
Phone: 212-558-5300
Fax: 212-344-5332
http://www.nul.org

Rainbow/PUSH Coalition
E-Mail: info@rainbowpush.org
1002 Wisconsin Ave. NW
Washington, D.C. 20007-3601
Phone: 202-333-5270
Fax: 202-728-1192
**http://www.rainbowpush.
org**

Concerned Women for
America
E-Mail: feedback form
1015 15th St. NW, Suite 1100
Washington, DC 20005
Phone: 202-488-7000
Fax: 202-488-0806
http://www.cwfa.org

Equal Rights Advocates
E-Mail: info@equalrights.org
1663 Mission St., Suite 250
San Francisco, CA 94103
Phone: 415-621-0672
Fax: 415-621-6744
http://www.equalrights.org

International Center for
Research on Women
E-Mail: info@icrw.org
1717 Massachusetts Ave. NW,
Suite 302
Washington, DC 20036
Phone: 202-797-0007
Fax: 202-797-0020
http://www.icrw.org

National Committee on Pay
Equity
E-mail: fairpay@patriot.net
1925 K St. NW, Suite 402
Washington, DC 20006-1119
Phone: 202-223-8360
Fax: 202-776-0537
http://www.pay-equity.org

National Partnership for
Women and Families
E-Mail: info@
nationalpartnership.org
1875 Connecticut Ave. NW,
Suite 650
Washington, DC 20009
Phone: 202-986-2600
Fax: 202-986-2539
http://www.
nationalpartnership.org

National Research Center for
Women and Families
1701 K St. NW, Suite 700
Washington, DC 20006
Phone: 202-223-4000
http://www.
center4research.org

National Women's Health
Network
514 10th St. NW, Suite 400
Washington DC 20004
Phone: 202-347-1140
Fax: 202-347-1168
http://www.
womenshealthnetwork.org

9to5, National Association of
Working Women
E-Mail: naww9to5@execpc.
com
231 W Wisconsin Ave., Suite
900
Milwaulkee, WI 53203-2308
Phone: 414-274-0925
Fax: 414-272-2870
http://www.9to5.org

National Center for Law and
Economic Justice
E-Mail: wlc@welfarelaw.org
275 Seventh Ave., Suite 1506
New York, NY 10001-6708
Phone: 212-633-6967
Fax: 212-633-6371
http://www.nclej.org

BIBLIOGRAPHY

Norton, David. *Nolo's Guide to Social Security Disability: Getting and Keeping Your Benefits*. 3rd ed. Berkeley. Nolo, 2006.

Johnson, Richard. *Work Impediments at Older Ages*. 2nd ed. Washington D.C.: Urban Institute, May 2006.

Peterson, Peter. *On Borrowed Time: How the growth in entitlement spending threatens America's future*. 2nd ed.. Washington D.C.: Transaction Publishers, 2004.

Epstein, Linda. *The Complete Idiot's Guide to Social Security and Medicare*. 2nd ed., New York: Penguin, 2006.

Davis, Mike. *How to Get SSI and Social Security Disability*. 1st ed. New York: Writers Club Press, 2000.

Conklin, Joan. Medicare *For The Clueless*. 1st ed., New York: Citadel Press, 2002.

The Library of Congress. 2007. 12 DEC 2007 **http://www.loc.gov/index.html.**

The Historical Background and Development of Social Security. 2008. 14 Jan 2008 **http://www.ssa.gov/history/history. html.**

Strengthening Social Security. 2 Jan 2008 **http://www. whitehouse.gov/infocus/social-security/.**

"Twelve Reasons Why Privatization Is a Bad Idea." 15 Dec 2007 **http://www.socsec.org/publications.asp?pubid=503.**

Social Security Disability: Frequently Asked Questions. 16 Dec 2007 **http://www.nosscr.org/faqind.html.**

The Social Security Handbook. 18 Apr 2006 17 Dec 2007 **http:// www.ssa.gov/OP_Home/handbook/.**

Hawes, Alexander. *The Consumer Law Page.* 18 Dec 2007 **http:// consumerlawpage.com/.**

Know Your Rights. 19 Dec 2007 **http://www.naca.net/know- your-consumer-rights/.**

"When Your Social Security Benefits Are Taken to Pay Back Money to the Federal Government." *Consumer Facts for Older Americans* 20 Dec 2008 **http://www.consumerlaw.org/ issues/seniors_initiative/ss_benefits.shtml.**

"Small Savings, Big Loss." *Health Care for All* 21 Dec 2007 **http:// hcfama.org/index.cfm?fuseaction=document.showDocume ntByID&DocumentID=67&varuniqueuserid=97821225676.**

ReferenceUSA. InfoUSA Company. 22 Dec 2007 **http://www. referenceusa.com/index2.asp?si=66260171214804.**

Callanan, Gerard and Greenhaus, Jefferey H. "The Baby Boom

Generation and Career Management: A Call to Action." *Sage Journals Online* vol. 10 (2008): pp. 70-85.

Rettenmaier, Andrew J. and Saving, Thomas R., "Medicare, Past, Present and Future." *National Center for Policy Analysis* 2323 Dec 2007 National Center for Policy Analysis.

Riedl, Brian M.. "Budget Resolution Calls for Massive Tax Hikes and Spending Increases." *Heritage Foundation* 44. 24 Dec 2007   **http://www.heritage.org/Research/Budget/upload/wm_1460.pdf.**

Fraser, Alison Acosta. "A Better Measure of Long-Term Spending: FASAB Proposes Changes in Accounting for Social Security, Medicare." *Heritage Foundation: Thomas A. Roe Instit Economic Policy Studies* 24 Dec 2007.

Brucker, "Demographic, employment, expenditure, and income-related dependency ratios: population aging in the fifty states." *Public Budgeting and Finance* vol. 26, no. 3 2006 pp. 65-80. 25 Dec 2007 **http://www-ca3.csa.com/ids70/view_record.php?id=2&recnum=4&log=from_res&SID=68af0abe14b5d450ea92e37ae5986b2d&mark_id=search%3A2%3A0%2C0%2C25.**

Shaw, Lois. "Differing Prospects For Women and Men: Young Old-Age, Old Old-Age, and Elder Care." vol 21Jul 2006 **http://www.levy.org/modules/pubslib/files/wp_464.pdf.**

Beach, William. "Public policy in the age of entitlements." Heritage Foundation May 2006. 26 Dec 2007 **http://www.heritage.org/Research/SocialSecurity/loader.cfm?url=/commonspot/security/getfile.cfm&PageID=95478.**

Marmor, Theodore. "Understanding Social Insurance: Fairness,

Affordability, and the 'Modernization' of Social Security and Medicare." *Health Affairs* (2006): pp. w114-w134.

Nunberg, Geoffrey. "Thinking about the government." *American Prospect* vol. 16(May 2005): pp. A8-A11.

Moore, Matt. "Social Security & Medicare forecast: 2005." Brief Analysis No. 510: *National Center for Policy Analysis* (Apr 2005).

"Reform should not wait for a crisis." *Concord Coalition* (Mar 2005): **http://www.concordcoalition.org/socialsecurity/ SSBrief1--Don't%20Wait%20for%20Crisis.pdf.**

Greenstein, Robert. "Administration expected to propose new budget rule that could adversely affect Social Security, Medicare, SSI, Veterans' disability, and other programs." *Center on Budget and Policy Priorities* Feb 2005 **http://www.cbpp. org/2-1-05bud.pdf.**

"Alan Greenspan on the economic implications of population aging." *Population and Development Review* vol. 30(Dec 2004.): pp. 779-783.

Janson, Bruce. "Empowering domestic discretionary spending in federal budget deliberations." *Social Policy Journal* vol. 1, no. 1(2002): pp. 5-18.

"America's Choice." *The Economist* vol. 357, no. 8195(Nov. 2000): pp. 27-29.

Feldstein, Martin. "The case for privatization." *Foreign Affairs* vol. 76(July/Aug.1997): pp. 24-38.

Simon, Julian. "Public expenditures on immigrants to the United States, past and present." *Population and Development Review* vol. 22(March 1996): pp. 99-109.

"Overview of entitlement programs: 1994 green book; background material and data on programs within the jurisdiction of the Committee on Ways and Means." *Superintendent of Documents* viii+1300 (1994).

"Aging issues: related GAO reports and activities in fiscal year 1989; report to the chairman, Special Committee on Aging, U.S. Senate." (1989): 63.

Trager, Oliver. *Poverty in America: the forgotten millions.* 2nd ed.. New York: Facts on File, 1989.

Braunstein, Jill. "Nonpartisan Medicare Information Available on National Academy of Social Insurance Website." *Health Reporter* 27 Dec 2007 **http://nasi.org/.**

Gardener, Amanda."Deciphering Medicare." *Health & Fitness* 42.

Gore, Al. "Policy Paper: Al Gore Would Use America's Prosperity to Strengthen and Modernize Medicare Highlights Makor Differences Between Gore and Bush Plans for Medicare." (Jul 2000).

Hinden, Stan. "A Senior's Health Care Wish List; Medicare's Prescription for Change Should Address Efficiency, Freedom of Choice." *Retirement Journal* Sept. 1998.

Craig Copeland, Employee Benefit Research Institute, EBRI Issue Brief no. 281 (May 2005), "Comparing Social Security Reform Options."

Williamson, John B., "Social Security Privatization: Lessons from the United Kingdom" (November 2000). BC Center for Retirement Research WP No. 2000-10. Available at SSRN: **http://ssrn. com/abstract=251705 or DOI: 10.2139/ssrn.251705.**

Gokhale, Jagadeesh., "The Impact of Social Security Reform on Low-Income Workers" (December 6, 2001). The CATO Institute. SSP No. 23. Available at **http://www.cato.org/pubs/ssps/ ssp23.pdf.**

"The History of Major Changes to the Social Security System," by Teresa T. King and Cecil H. Wayne, The CPA Journal, May 2006.

Hacker, Jacob S. Ph.D. *The Divided Welfare State: The Battle over Public and Private Social Benefits in the United States* (Cambridge University Press, 2002).

Edwards, Alejandra Cox; Estelle James; and Rebeca Wong. "The Impact of Social Security Reform on Women in Three Countries". National Center for Policy Analysis, Policy Report No. 264, November 4, 2003.

www.wiserwomen.org/pdf_files/senatetestimony_final.pdf

www.medicare.gov/

www.medicare.org/

www.lexisnexis.com/us/lnacademic/auth/checkbrowser.do ?ipcounter=1&cookieState=0&rand=0.3039904880370284 4&bhcp=1

www.ryanalm.com/Portals/5/newsletters/ Commentary_2007_12.pdf

http://web.ebscohost.com/ehost/search?vid=1&hid=8&sid=66e9e9c9-84f2-4920-ae54-2cc57320d7ec%40sessionmgr9

http://find.galegroup.com/itx/start.do?prodId=AONE&userGroupName=orla57816&finalAuth=true

http://library.cqpress.com/cqresearcher/

www.heritage.org/Research/SocialSecurity/wm726.cfm

www.cms.hhs.gov

www.apapractice.org/apo/insider/practice/pracmanage/practice_management/dsm-9.html#

www.apapractice.org/apo/insider/practice/working_with_medicare/quadruple.html#

http://oig.hhs.gov/oei/reports/oei-03-99-00130.pdf

www.aarp.org/research/medicare/financing/the_medicare_program_a_brief_overview.htm

www.ama-assn.org/ama/pub/category/3113.html

www.nzhis.govt.nz/documentation/mapping/icd9-dsmiv.html

www.empiremedicare.com/newypolicy/policy/ps001e%5Ffinal.htm

http://ks.webjunction.org/do/DisplayContent?id=16747

www.galorath.com/customer_case-ssa.html

http://macroblog.typepad.com/macroblog/2004/11/argentina_chile.html

http://govinfo.library.unt.edu/npr/library/studies/ssa.pdf

http://bnetworks.blogspot.com/2007/08/new-study-takes-fresh-look-at-value-of.html

www.sciencedirect.com/science?_ob=ArticleURL&_udi=B6W4G-43MBV7P-6&_user=2139851&_rdoc=1&_fmt=&_orig=search&_sort=d&view=c&_acct=C000054275&_version=1&_urlVersion=0&_userid=2139851&md5=5731867fb2b259116795899b836c48b4

www.compassrosebenefits.com/medicare.html

http://www.medicare.gov/LongTermCare/Static/LTCInsurance.asp?dest=NAV%7CPaying%7CPrivateInsurance

http://consumerlawpage.com

www.naca.net

www.nclc.org

www.calmedicare.org

www.ladpss.org/dpss/health_care/aged_blind_disabled/medicare_reimbursement.cfm

www.healthlaw.org

www.healthcarerights.org

http://hcfama.org

https://nppes.cms.hhs.gov

www.historycentral.com.

www.ssa.gov/

www.genealogytoday.com/guide/help/ssa.html

www.loc.gov/index.html

www.whitehouse.gov/infocus/social-security/

www.socyberty.com/Government/The-History-of-Social-Security-and-its-Future-.44389

www.basicsproject.org/social_security_reform/history_of_social_security_in_the_us.htm

www.socsec.org/publications.asp?pubid=503

www.socialsecurity.gov/retire2/near.htm

www.aarp.org/money/social_security/

www.nolo.com/resource.cfm/catID/A74E92D1-EE6C-420C-B64B7FCB6A2953A8/213/233/

www.ultimatedisabilityguide.com/

www.4socialsecuritydisability.net/

www.nosscr.org/faqind.html

www.socialsecurity.gov/woundedwarriors/

www.disabilityinfo.gov/digov-public/public/DisplayPage.do?parentFolderId=500

http://money.cnn.com/2004/04/06/pf/expert/ask_
expert/index.htm

www.irs.gov/faqs/faq6.html

http://en.allexperts.com/q/Disability-Law-917/Lump-sum-
payment-receiving.htm

http://en.allexperts.com/q/Disability-Law-917/disabilty-
lump-sum-payment.htm

http://public.findlaw.com/bookshelf-ssa-handbook/
handbook.09/handbook-toc09.html

www.socialsecurity.gov/employer/ssnv.htm

www.socialsecurity.gov/employer/critical.htm

www.floridajobs.org/unemployment/index.html

workforcesecurity.doleta.gov/unemploy

www.edd.ca.gov

www.dol.gov

http://law.jrank.org/pages/6812/Federal-Unemployment-
Compensation-Act.html

www.nelp.org/ui

www.epinet.org

http://research.lawyers.com/State-Unemployment-
Insurance-Websites.html

www.fldfs.com/wc/faq/faqwrkrs.html

http://boardreader.com/tp/unemployment+compensation+florida.html

www.acf.hhs.gov/programs/ofa/

www.fns.usda.gov/fsp/ebt/

www.fns.usda.gov/wic/

www.acf.hhs.gov/programs/liheap/

www.fns.usda.gov/fdd/programs/tefap/

www.nectac.org/partc/partc.asp

www.fns.usda.gov/cnd/milk/

www.ed.gov/programs/rsailob/index.html

www.freedomfromhunger.org/

www.salvationarmyusa.org/usn/www_usn.nsf

www.rxassist.org

www.pparx.org

www.gsa.gov/Portal/gsa/ep/home.do?tabId=0

www.pbgc.gov/

www.mymoney.gov/

http://thomas.loc.gov/

www.medicare.gov/

www.senate.gov/

www.disabilitysecrets.com/

www.rabinsslaw.com/

http://disabilityblogger.blogspot.com/2007/01/appealing-denied-disability-claim.html

www.lechtmanlaw.com/PracticeAreas/Social-Security-Disability-Claims.asp

www.gabinlawoffice.com/lawyer-attorney-1179442.html

www.simolikelaw.com/PracticeAreas/Social-Security-Disability.asp

www.rosenfeld.com/PracticeAreas/Social-Security-Disability-Claims.asp

www.seniormag.com/legal/disability-claim.htm

www.employee-advocates.com/PracticeAreas/Social-Security-Disability.asp

www.socialsecurityhome.com/

http://law.freeadvice.com/insurance_law/disability_insurance/denied_disabilty_benefits.htm

AUTHOR DEDICATION & BIOGRAPHY

This book is for the people...

*"I am a firm believer in the people. If given the truth,
they can be depended upon to meet any national crisis.
The great point is to bring them the real facts."*

Abraham Lincoln

Along-time resident of Central Florida, Vaughnlea Leonard graduated from the University of Central Florida with a B.A. in English. Her undergraduate coursework included: Economics, Statistics, Journalism, Modern Literary and Advanced Feminist Theory, Social, and Religious Philosophy. While attending UCF's Interdisciplinary Studies graduate program, Ms. Leonard studied Modern and Gendered Rhetoric, Social Theory, Advanced Ethics, and Philosophy.

As a working single mother, Ms. Leonard first became interested in Social Security more than 15 years ago when her first child became disabled as an infant. After her second child was born with similar medical difficulties, Ms. Leonard began talking with others about their own difficulties within the system.

During her university attendance, Ms. Leonard worked as a daily laborer, construction worker, pool builder, waitress, maid, street cleaner, secretary, and commercial janitor. After graduating from college in 2005, she worked as an English instructor and newspaper reporter.

She currently works as a freelance writer and lives in Central Florida with her two children.

INDEX